W9-BNS-042

∏B   The Practitioner's Bookshelf

Hands-On Literacy Books for
Classroom Teachers and Administrators

Dorothy S. Strickland
FOUNDING EDITOR, LANGUAGE AND LITERACY SERIES

Donna E. Alvermann and Celia Genishi
LANGUAGE AND LITERACY SERIES EDITORS*

Teaching Individual Words:
One Size Does Not Fit All
Michael F. Graves

Literacy Essentials for English Language Learners:
Successful Transitions
Maria Uribe and Sally Nathenson-Mejía

Literacy Leadership in Early Childhood:
The Essential Guide
Dorothy S. Strickland and Shannon Riley-Ayers

* For a list of current titles in the Language and Literacy Series, see *www.tcpress.com*

Teaching
Individual Words

ONE SIZE DOES NOT FIT ALL

MICHAEL F. GRAVES

Foreword by James F. Baumann

Teachers College
Columbia University
New York and London

INTERNATIONAL
Reading Association
800 BARKSDALE ROAD, PO BOX 8139
NEWARK, DE 19714-8139, USA (302) 731-1600
www.reading.org

Published simultaneously by Teachers College Press, 1234 Amsterdam Avenue, New York, NY 10027 and The International Reading Association, 800 Barksdale Road, P.O. Box 8139, Newark, DE 19714-8139

Library of Congress Cataloging-in-Publication Data

Graves, Michael F.
  Teaching individual words: one size does not fit all / Michael F. Graves; foreword by James Bauman.
        p. cm.—(The practitioner's bookshelf)
  Includes bibliographical references and index.
  ISBN 978-0-8077-4930-2 (pbk.)
1. Vocabulary—Study and teaching (Elementary) I. Title.
  LB1574.5.G718 2009
  372.6—dc22   2008032902

ISBN 978-0-8077-4930-2 (paper)

IRA inventory number 9189

Printed on acid-free paper
Manufactured in the United States of America

16 15 14 13 12 11 10 09   8 7 6 5 4 3 2 1

Again, to Bonnie

Contents

Foreword by James F. Baumann   ix

1.   Introduction   1
    The Importance of Vocabulary   2
    The Vocabularies of Linguistically Less Advantaged Children   3
    A Comprehensive Four-Part Vocabulary Program   5
    The Focus of This Book   8

2.   Crucial Facts About Words and Word Learning   10
    How Many Vocabularies Do We Have?   11
    What Is a Word?   11
    What Does It Mean To "Know" a Word?   12
    How Many Words Are There?   13
    How Many Words Do Students Learn?   14
    How Do Word-Learning Tasks Differ?   15
    Summing Up   18

3.   Common Considerations for Vocabulary Instruction   19
    The Frequency Distribution of English Words   20
    Selecting Vocabulary to Teach   23
    Principles of Effective Vocabulary Instruction   27
    The Importance of Student-Friendly Definitions   29
    Special Consideration for English Learners   30
    Summing Up   32

4.   Building Students' Oral Vocabularies   33
    Approaches for All Students   34
    An Approach for Students with Small Vocabularies   37
    Summing Up   45

5.   Rich and Powerful Instruction   46
    Semantic Mapping   47
    Semantic Feature Analysis   48

Four Squares   51
Venn Diagrams   52
Vocabulary Self-Collection Strategy   55
Possible Sentences   56
Focused Discussion   57
Vocabulary Visits   58
Robust Instruction   60
Knowledge as Design   62
Frayer Method   63
Expressive Vocabulary Instruction   66
Summing Up   68

6.   Introductory Instruction   69
Teaching Students to Read Known Words   70
Providing Glossaries   70
Context-Dictionary-Discussion   72
Definition Plus Rich Context   72
Definition, Rich Context, and a Picture   73
Context-Relationship   74
Teaching New Meanings for Known Words   75
Summing Up   77

**7.   Repetition, Assessment, and Differences
        Across Grade Levels   79**
The Importance of Repetition   80
Assessing Word Knowledge   85
Differences Across Grade Levels   90
Final Comments   92

References and Children's Literature   93

Index   101

About the Author   107

Foreword

Does the world need another book on vocabulary instruction? This might seem to be an odd way to begin a foreword to a book on vocabulary. But if one looks at the increased attention to vocabulary instruction in the past 10 years and the proliferation of books on the topic, this question may not be so absurd.

The answer? Well, it depends. The answer is "no" if one refers to an idea or strategy book that provides a potpourri of vocabulary instruction techniques. We have plenty of those—and lots of good ones. However, the answer is "yes" if one refers to a book that fills a void in our library on vocabulary issues, and that's exactly what *Teaching Individual Words* does.

In his prior work, *The Vocabulary Book* (2006), Mike Graves articulated a framework for conceptualizing and implementing a vocabulary instruction program; this useful structure has guided me and others in research, program development, and teaching. In *Teaching Individual Words*, however, Mike provides needed elaboration and extension of one of those four key components: how to instruct students in specific words. To a certain extent all vocabulary books do this, but *Teaching Individual Words* examines in detail the rationale for, importance of, and strategies for teaching individual words to expand students' vocabularies. This focus has resulted in a number of unique features that are not addressed well or at all in other books on vocabulary instruction:

- *Goals for word learning.* Mike examines the varied goals of word learning, which include learning a basic oral vocabulary, learning new words that represent known concepts, learning new words that represent entirely new concepts, and learning new meanings for known words.
- *Selecting words to teach.* How to decide which words to teach is a persistent, vexing problem teachers face. Mike provides a co-

gent set of 5 questions teachers can ask to determine which words should be taught given the text at hand and their instructional goals.

• *Vocabulary instruction for English learners.* Students learning English as a second language need special consideration when teachers design and implement vocabulary instruction. This critical issue is addressed by expressing several principles for teaching English learners, delineating a set of general accommodations for teaching vocabulary to English learners, and specifying specific accommodations for teaching individual words to English learners.

• *Oral vocabulary instruction.* For native-speaking students coming to school with limited vocabularies and for English learners, it is essential that teachers broaden their oral vocabularies. Mike provides specific approaches and strategies for this oft-ignored aspect of vocabulary instruction.

• *Rich and powerful instruction.* For students to acquire sophisticated understandings of key words, teachers must conduct ambitious, elaborate lessons. Mike provides various strategies for teaching word meanings in ways that students will acquire deep, nuanced conceptual understandings.

• *Introductory instruction.* Students also must be exposed to many words. This will enable them to acquire a basic understanding of words for an immediate purpose and it will lay the groundwork for a subsequent deepening of understanding of those words. Mike provides a series of engaging and effective strategies for providing students with this "foot-in-the-door" level of word knowledge.

• *Assessing word knowledge.* Teachers need to be able to gauge students' knowledge of individual words. Mike provides several clever, efficient, and valid ways for teachers assess the meanings of specific words.

So, does the world need another book on vocabulary instruction? Yes, it needs this one, for no other text available addresses in detail how teachers can select, teach, and assess the meanings of specific words. In order for students to acquire a common vocabulary, they need to learn many specific words. *Teaching Individual Words* provides educators the means to achieve that goal.

James F. Baumann
University of Wyoming

CHAPTER 1

Introduction

At age 7 in a magical moment, something truly wonderful happened to Helen Keller, who had been deaf, blind, and almost totally isolated from the world since a mysterious illness when she was 1½ years old. Helen recognized that the word *water*, which Anne Sullivan was finger-spelling in her hand, represented the water that she felt coming from the pump in her yard.

Through this singular event, Helen learned that things in her dark, silent world had names and discovered a way to communicate, to again become a part of the world. Once having made this break-through, Helen made astounding progress, mastering writing and becoming relatively accomplished in speech. Five years later, she published her first magazine article, and 5 years after that, she entered Radcliffe College, graduating cum laude 4 years later. Over the next 60 years, Helen became a world-renowned author and champion for the blind, women's suffrage, and other causes; and in 1964 President Lyndon Johnson conferred the Presidential Medal of Freedom, the nation's highest civilian honor, on her.

Few children experience the deprivation that Helen experienced, and even fewer overcome that deprivation to become world-famous authors and lecturers. But all children, indeed all human beings, benefit tremendously from learning the words of their language. As Ludwig Wittgenstein (1953) once noted, "The limits of my language are the limits of my mind. All I know is what I have words for." This book is about teaching words and in doing so expanding the limits of children's minds. More specifically, this book describes one part of a comprehensive vocabulary program—teaching individual words. In the remainder of this chapter, I discuss the importance of vocabulary, the vocabularies of linguistically less advantaged students, the four parts of a comprehensive vocabulary program, and the focus of this book.

THE IMPORTANCE OF VOCABULARY

The importance of vocabulary is attested to by a plethora of authorities. In an early and somewhat prosaic statement—but one I see as both comprehensive and irrefutable—Petty, Herold, and Stoll (1967) said this:

> The importance of vocabulary is daily demonstrated in schools and out. In the classroom, the achieving students possess the most adequate vocabularies. Because of the verbal nature of most classroom activities, knowledge of words and ability to use language are essential to success in these activities. After schooling has ended, adequacy of vocabulary is almost equally essential for achievement in vocations and in society. (p. 7)

More recently and more poetically, Stahl and Stahl (2004) observed that "to expand a child's vocabulary is to teach that child to think about the world." And more recently still, Phythian-Sence and Wagner (2007) began a book on vocabulary acquisition by noting that "acquiring the vocabulary we use for thinking and communicating is a linguistic achievement of nearly incomprehensible importance and complexity."

The importance of vocabulary is also attested to by a huge body of empirical evidence (see Graves, 1986, 2006, 2007). Among the data-based claims that can be made about word knowledge are these:

- Vocabulary knowledge in kindergarten and first grade is a significant predictor of reading comprehension in the middle and secondary grades.
- Vocabulary difficulty strongly influences the readability of text.
- The vocabulary we use strongly influences judgments of our competence.
- Teaching vocabulary can improve reading comprehension.
- Growing up in poverty can seriously restrict the vocabulary children learn before beginning school and make attaining an adequate vocabulary a very challenging task.
- Learning English vocabulary is one of the most crucial tasks for English learners.
- Lack of vocabulary can be a crucial factor underlying the school failure of many students.

Of course, in addition to the testimony of experts and empirical evidence, common sense and our own experiences as teachers and language users testifies to the importance of vocabulary. Possessing and using a powerful vocabulary helps us better understand others, be better understood by others, and enjoy the richness of the English language.

THE VOCABULARIES OF LINGUISTICALLY LESS ADVANTAGED CHILDREN

The vocabulary instruction described in this book is important for all students—to those with small vocabularies, who desperately need to learn words to succeed in school; to those with average vocabularies, who need to learn more words to become productive and successful members of our society; and to those with exceptional vocabularies, who need to become even more skillful word learners to reach even higher levels of success. But vocabulary instruction is particularly important for linguistically less advantaged students, students with vocabularies considerably smaller than those of their peers. These include many students of poverty, many English learners, and many less able readers.

Based on a review of research completed nearly 40 years ago, Carroll (1971) noted that "much of the failure of individuals to understand speech or writing beyond an elementary level is due to deficiencies in vocabulary knowledge."

In an influential article published some years later, Becker (1977) considered what we learned from both the failures and successes of Project Follow Through, the federal program designed to test ways of improving first- through third-grade disadvantaged students' school success. These results indicated that none of the nine Follow Through projects resulted in students scoring above expectations on tests of word meaning and comprehension. Becker attributed this failure to the fact that both these Follow Through projects and schools more generally "fail to provide instruction in the building blocks crucial to intelligent functioning, namely, words and their referents."

Somewhat more recently, two colleagues and I (White, Graves, & Slater, 1990) investigated the vocabularies of first- through fourth-grade students in three schools—a suburban school enrolling middle-class White students who spoke standard English; an inner-city school enrolling dialect-speaking Black students of lower socioeconomic status (SES); and a semi-rural school enrolling lower-SES, dialect-speaking Asian/Pacific students. Results showed that fourth graders in the two lower-SES schools knew about 13,000 words while those in the middle-class school knew about 19,000 words. Results further showed that in grades 1 to 3 the rate of vocabulary growth for middle-class students was about one and a half times that for lower-SES students.

At this same time, Chall, Jacobs, and Baldwin (1990; see also Chall & Jacobs, 2003) published their study of why and when poor children fall behind in school. What they found is that the low-income children in their study did about as well as the general population in grades 2 and 3 but began to fall behind in grade 4 and continued to fall further behind in grades 5 and 6. The first and strongest factor to show a decline was knowledge of word meanings. By the end of grade 4, the low-income children had fallen about a year behind, and by the end of grade 6, they had fallen about 2 years behind.

More recently, Hart and Risley (1995; see also 2003) published their longitudinal study of the vocabularies of 1- to 3-year-old children of professional, working-class, and welfare families. There results showed that by the time they were 3, the children from the welfare families had heard 30 million fewer words than had those from the professional families. As a result of this lack of exposure, the children from welfare families knew less than half as many words as those from professional families. Results further showed that these differences persisted into kindergarten and beyond that into third grade, the last year in which the children were tested.

As Biemiller and Boote (2006) have pointed out, schools currently do little to close the gap in oral vocabulary between linguistically more advantaged and linguistically less advantaged students. Clearly, this is a problem we need to address.

A COMPREHENSIVE FOUR-PART VOCABULARY PROGRAM

Over the past 25 years, I have worked to develop a comprehensive vocabulary program—one broad enough to accommodate children who enter school with relatively small vocabularies, English learners with small English vocabularies, children who possess adequate but not exceptional vocabularies, and children who already have rich and powerful vocabularies and are prepared for the challenge of developing still more sophisticated and useful vocabularies (see, for example, Graves, 1984, 1985, 1987, 1992, 2000, 2004, 2006, 2007). In its present form—described in detail in Graves (2006)—the program has the following four components: providing frequent, varied, and extensive language experiences; teaching individual words; teaching word-learning strategies; and fostering word consciousness. In the next several paragraphs, I briefly describe each component.

Providing Frequent, Varied, and Extensive Language Experiences

One way to build students' vocabularies is to immerse them in a rich array of language experiences so that they learn words through listening, speaking, reading, and writing. In kindergarten and the primary grades, listening and speaking are particularly important for promoting vocabulary growth. Most children enter kindergarten with substantial oral vocabularies and very small reading vocabularies. Appropriately, most of the words in materials they read are words that are in their oral vocabularies. For this reason, young children will not learn many new words from reading. Where they will learn them is from discussion, from being read to, and from having attention directly focused on words.

In the intermediate and middle grades, discussion continues to be important. Students of all ages and English learners as well as native English speakers need to engage frequently in authentic discussions—give-and-take conversations in which they have the opportunity to thoughtfully discuss topics. Increasingly, though, from the intermediate grades on, reading becomes the principal language experience for increasing students' vocabularies. If we can substantially increase the reading that intermediate-grade students do, we can substantially increase the words they learn.

Thus, anyone interested in increasing primary-grade students' vocabularies should do everything possible to see that they listen to selections with rich vocabulary and engage in discussion of meaty topics, while those interested in increasing intermediate- and middle-grade students' vocabularies should do both of these and ensure that students read as much and as widely as possible.

Teaching Individual Words

Another way to help students increase their vocabularies is of course to teach them individual words. Fortunately, research is extremely informative in revealing effective—and ineffective—approaches to teaching individual words. Vocabulary instruction is most effective when it is rich, deep, and extended. However, because there are a huge number of words students need to learn, because there are different levels of word knowledge that we can attempt to build in students, and because there are a variety of word-learning tasks, not all vocabulary instruction can or should be rich, deep, and extended. Detailing why and how to use different sorts of instruction for these different circumstances—explaining why one-size vocabulary instruction does not fit all and describing various sorts of instruction—is the purpose of this book.

Teaching Word-Learning Strategies

A third approach to help students increase their vocabularies is to teach word-learning strategies. The most widely recommended strategy is that of using context to infer the meanings of unknown words. Using word parts to unlock the meanings of unknown words is another widely recommended strategy. Using the dictionary is a third recommended approach. And for Spanish speakers, using cognates (words that sound about the same, are spelled about the same, and mean much the same thing in two languages) is another recommended approach.

Fostering Word Consciousness

The last component of the four-part program is fostering word consciousness. The term *word consciousness* refers to an awareness of and interest in words and their meanings. Word consciousness involves both a cognitive and an affective stance toward words. It integrates metacognition about words, motivation to learn words, and deep and lasting interest in words. Students who are word conscious are aware of the words around them—those they read and hear and those they write and speak. This awareness involves an appreciation of the power of words, an understanding of why certain words are used instead of others, and a sense of the words that could be used in place of those selected by a writer or speaker. It also involves recognition of the communicative power of words, of the differences between spoken and written language, and of the particular importance of word choice in written language. And it involves an interest in learning and using new words and becoming more skillful and precise in word usage. Word consciousness exists at many levels of complexity and sophistication, and it can and should be fostered at all grade levels.

As I have noted, each of these four parts of a comprehensive vocabulary program is described in some detail in *The Vocabulary Book* (Graves, 2006).

THE FOCUS OF THIS BOOK

Having just said that a comprehensive vocabulary program consists of four parts, the fact that this book deals with only one of
them deserves explanation. There are two reasons. First, although
each part of the four-part program is important, teaching individual words is truly central to vocabulary instruction. When we
first think about teaching vocabulary, that is what we think about
doing. Second, while we know a lot about all types of vocabulary
instruction, we know a really huge amount about what constitutes
effective instruction in individual words. This book presents that
information, with lots of practical examples.

In addition to this overview chapter, this book contains six chapters, each of which is briefly described here. Chapter 2 begins with
discussions of the different types of vocabulary each of us learns,
what unit I will refer to as a word, and the levels of word knowledge we can achieve. The discussion then focuses on the number of
words in American English, how many words students learn, and
the different learning tasks that various words present.

Chapter 3 discusses common considerations for all types of vocabulary instruction. These include the frequency distribution of
English words, selecting vocabulary to teach, principles of effective
vocabulary instruction, the importance of student-friendly definitions, and special considerations for English learners.

Chapter 4 begins with a discussion of approaches to fostering
oral vocabulary appropriate for all students. These approaches include your reading aloud from quality children's literature, your
deliberately using some sophisticated vocabulary in your speech,
your complimenting and encouraging students' use of adept word
choices, and your involving students in discussion of sophisticated
topics that invite sophisticated words. The chapter closes with a
description of an approach specifically designed to increase the oral
vocabularies of students with small vocabularies, a procedure often
called shared book reading.

Chapter 5 describes vocabulary instruction that leaves students
with deep and lasting knowledge of the words taught. It begins
with a review of characteristics of effective vocabulary instruction, followed by descriptions and examples of a dozen methods
of powerful vocabulary instruction. The chapter concludes with

a reminder that powerful vocabulary instruction is also time-consuming instruction.

Because there is also a place for admittedly less powerful but also less time-consuming instruction, Chapter 6 describes and gives examples of seven less time-consuming methods.

Chapter 7 begins with a discussion of the importance of repetition and reviews and describes four procedures for reviewing words. Next, it describes several assessments you may want to use in your classroom. After that, it describes some differences in vocabulary instruction as you move from the primary grades, to the intermediate grades, and on to middle school.

Taken as a whole, this book will enable you to create effective, efficient, and engaging instruction on individual words. While no single word you teach is likely to have the life-changing effect that learning *water* had for Helen Keller, each word students learn will, as it did for Wittgenstein, expand the limits of their minds.

CHAPTER 2

Crucial Facts About
Words and Word Learning

This chapter explains some basic facts about vocabulary, facts that underlie the instructional approaches described in the remaining chapters in this book. Understanding these facts will enable you to build on the information in this book to create your own powerful vocabulary instruction. In the next few pages, I discuss the different types of vocabulary each of us learns, what unit I will refer to as a "word," the levels of word knowledge we can achieve, how many words there are in American English, how many words students learn, and the different learning tasks that different words present.

HOW MANY VOCABULARIES DO WE HAVE?

It is important to recognize that we have several different vocabularies and to distinguish among these types. Vocabulary can be classified as receptive (words we understand when others use them) and productive (words we use ourselves). Vocabulary can also be classified as oral or written. Thus, each of us has four vocabularies:

- Words we understand when we hear them
- Words we can read
- Words we use in our speech
- Words we use in our writing

The four vocabularies overlap but are not the same, and the relationships between them change over time.

Although some children come to school with much smaller vocabularies than others, all children entering school have relatively large oral vocabularies but quite small (perhaps nonexistent) reading vocabularies. Sometime during the upper-elementary years, good readers' reading vocabularies begin to outstrip their oral vocabularies, and literate adults have larger reading vocabularies than oral vocabularies. Additionally, both children and adults have larger receptive vocabularies than productive ones; that is, we understand more words than we use in our speech or writing.

The primary emphasis in this book will be on reading vocabulary; but I will also give a good deal of attention to listening vocabulary, since it is vital that we build the listening vocabularies of children who arrive at school with small vocabularies.

WHAT IS A WORD?

Philosophers, linguists, and educators have grappled over a considerable period of time with the question of what constitutes a word, and it is certainly not my goal to answer that question in a definitive way here. Instead, I want to explain how the term will be used in this book, particularly in discussions of how many words students know or need to learn. When written, words are groups of letters separated by white space. Thus, *the* is a word, *apple* another

word, *predawn* another, *perpendicular* another, and *houseboat* still
another. By this same definition, *want, wants, wanted,* and *wanting*
are also words. However, for the most part, when I am considering
how many words students know or need to learn, I will use the
term *word* to refer to *word families.* By *word families,* I mean the basic
word and its inflected forms. Thus, when I say that children add
something like 3,000 words to their reading vocabularies each year
they are in school, I will be counting the forms *want, wants, wanted,*
and *wanting* as a single word.

Another convention I will follow in talking about vocabulary
size is to count graphic forms with different meanings as a single
word. Thus, *key* referring to a door key, *key* the musical term, and
key meaning a small island are considered one word. Doing so definitely underestimates the size of the learning task, but it is necessary because almost all studies of vocabulary size count the number of graphic forms in the language without considering whether
or not they represent different meanings.

WHAT DOES IT MEAN TO "KNOW" A WORD?

A number of vocabulary scholars have considered the various levels of word knowledge a learner can achieve, and they are all in
agreement on one matter: Words can be known at various levels.
For example, Beck, McKeown, and Kucan (2002, p. 10) list five levels. Below is a slightly modified version of their levels.

- No knowledge
- General sense, such as knowing *mendacious* has a negative
  connotation
- Narrow, context-bound knowledge, such as knowing that
  a *radiant* bride is a beautifully smiling and happy one,
  but being unable to describe an individual in a different
  context as "radiant"
- Having a basic knowledge of a word and being able to use
  the word in a variety of appropriate situations
- Having a rich, decontextualized knowledge of a word's
  meaning, its relationship to other words, and its extension
  to metaphorical uses, such as understanding what
  someone is doing when they are "devouring" a book

This scale make good sense, and it is something to keep in mind as you plan instruction. Still, there is more to be said about what it means to know a word. Some years ago, Cronbach (1942) noted that knowing a word involves the ability to select situations in which it is appropriately applied, recall different meanings of the word, and recognize in just which situations the word does and does not apply. More recently, Calfee and Drum (1986) noted that knowing a word well "involves depth of meaning; precision of meaning; facile access (think of scrabble and crossword puzzle experts); the ability to articulate one's understanding; flexibility in the application of the knowledge of a word; the appreciation of metaphor, analogy, word play; the ability to recognize a synonym, to define, to use a word expressively."

Nagy and Scott (2000) further underscore the complexity of what it means to know a word when they discuss several aspects of word knowledge, including incrementality, polysemy, interrelatedness, and heterogeneity. We learn word meanings *incrementally*, learning something about a word's meaning the first time we meet it, something more the second time, and so on. Many words are *polysemous*, that is, they have multiple meanings. Word meanings are *interrelated* in such a way that a learner's knowledge of one word is linked to his or her knowledge of other words. To use Nagy and Scott's example, "A person who already knows the words *hot, cold,* and *cool* has already acquired some of the components of the word *warm,* even if the word *warm* has not yet been encountered." Finally, word knowledge is *heterogeneous* in that what it means to know a word is dependent on the type of word in question. Knowing function words such as *the* or *if* is quite different from knowing concrete nouns like *ladder*, and knowing concrete nouns like *ladder* is quite different from knowing abstract terms like *democracy*.

HOW MANY WORDS ARE THERE?

In the most serious attempt to get a reliable estimate of how many words there are in contemporary American English, Nagy and Anderson completed a study appropriately titled "How Many Words Are There in Printed School English?" (1984). They investigated the number of words in printed school English using as their source *The American Heritage Word Frequency Book* (Carroll, Davies, & Rich-

man, 1971), a very well done compilation of the words occurring
in books and other material likely to be used by children in grades
3–9. Based on careful study and a number of calculations, Nagy and
Anderson concluded that printed school English contains about
88,000 word families. Subsequent to the original study, Anderson
and Nagy (1992) again considered the vocabulary size of printed
school English and concluded that if proper nouns, multiple meanings of words, and idioms were included, their estimate would increase to 180,000 word families.

More recently, Zeno, Ivens, Millard, and Duvvuri produced the
The Educator's Word Frequency Guide (1995), basically an updated
version of the *Word Frequency Book* based on a much larger corpus
of material used in kindergarten through college. Although no one
has yet calculated the number of word families in the *The Educator's
Word Frequency Guide*, since the number of entries in the *Guide* is
considerably larger than the number in the *Word Frequency Book*, it
is reasonable to assume that an estimate based on the *Guide* would
be well over 180,000.

Note that these are not estimates of the size of individual students' vocabularies; they are estimates of the number of words that
appear in the myriad texts students might encounter. Note also that
many of these words are extremely rare and that no single student
will encounter all of them, much less learn all of them. Still, it is
important to realize that there are this many words that might be
taught. It is very clear that we cannot teach all of them, and we
therefore need to be very selective in choosing those to teach.

HOW MANY WORDS DO STUDENTS LEARN?

Estimates of the number of words in students' reading vocabularies
vary considerably. They range from lows of 2,000 words for third
graders and 7,800 words for twelfth graders (Dupuy, 1974) to highs
of 26,000 words for first graders (Shibles, 1959) and over 200,000
words for college freshmen (Hartman, 1946). These extreme estimates can be dismissed or at least very strongly questioned because
of such factors as the size of the dictionary from which words were
sampled, the definition of what constitutes a word, the method of
testing, the sampling procedures used, and such ad hoc require-
ments as that a word appear in a number of different dictionaries
(Graves, 1986; Lorge & Chall, 1963).

The most unbiased estimate of the size of students' reading vocabularies comes, in my judgment, from work done by Nagy and Herman (1987; see also Stahl & Nagy, 2006, Chapter 3). Using data gathered from Nagy and Anderson's 1984 study, Nagy and Herman recalibrated earlier estimates and concluded that third graders' reading vocabularies average about 10,000 words, that twelfth graders' reading vocabularies average about 40,000 words, and that schoolchildren therefore learn about 3,000 words each year. These figures refer to word families as previously described, but they do not include idioms, multiple meanings, or proper nouns, which would raise the figure considerably. Recent estimates by experts are in the same general range as Nagy and Herman's estimate but somewhat higher. Snow and Kim (2007), for example, recently suggested that high school graduates need to know 75,000 words.

All in all, my best estimate (based on the work of Anderson & Nagy, 1992; Anglin, 1993; Miller & Wakefield, 1993; Nagy & Anderson, 1984; Nagy & Herman, 1987; and White, Graves, & Slater, 1990) is that average students learn words at the rate of 3,000 to 4,000 word families each year, resulting in average eighth graders knowing something like 35,000 word families and average twelfth graders knowing something like 50,000 word families. These figures, however, are for average or above-average students. As previously noted, a number of studies (for example, Biemiller & Slonim, 2001; Hart & Risley, 1995; Templin, 1957; White et al., 1990) have demonstrated large differences between the vocabularies of linguistically advantaged and linguistically disadvantaged students. A reasonable estimate is that linguistically advantaged students enter first grade with an oral vocabulary of perhaps 10,000 words and leave high school with a reading and oral vocabulary in the 50,000 word range, while linguistically disadvantaged students both enter and leave school with vocabularies of about half that size. Obviously, our goal is to help all students develop extensive vocabularies— something like 50,000 words—over the school years.

HOW DO WORD-LEARNING TASKS DIFFER?

It is important to realize that all word-learning tasks are not the same; in fact, the task of learning a word can vary a great deal from one word to the other. Word-learning tasks differ depending on such matters as the conceptual difficulty of the words, how much students already know about the words, how well you want them to learn the words, and what you want them to be able to do with the words afterwards. Here, I consider seven tasks students face in learning words, some of which are quite different from others and require quite different sorts of instruction.

Learning a Basic Oral Vocabulary

As noted, many children arrive at school with substantial oral vocabularies, perhaps numbering 10,000 words. However, some linguistically disadvantaged children come to school with meager oral vocabularies; and, of course, some English learners come to school with very limited English vocabularies. For such children, building a basic oral vocabulary of the most frequent English words is of utmost importance. Because learning a basic oral vocabulary is so important, I discuss it at length in Chapter 4.

Learning to Read Known Words

Learning to read known words, words that are already in their oral vocabularies, is the major vocabulary learning task of beginning readers. Such words as *surprise*, *stretch*, and *amaze* are ones that students might be taught to read during their first 3 years of school. By third or fourth grade, good readers will have learned to read most of the words in their oral vocabularies. However, the task of learning to read many of the words in their oral vocabularies remains for many less proficient readers and for some English learners.

Learning New Words Representing Known Concepts

A third word-learning task students face is learning to read words that are in neither their oral nor their reading vocabularies but for which they have an available concept. For example, the word *goulash* meaning a type of stew would be unknown to a number of third graders. Similarly, the word *ensemble* meaning a group of musicians would be an unknown word for many eighth graders. But in both cases the concepts are familiar. All students continue to learn words of this sort throughout their years in school, making this one of the major word-learning tasks students face. It is also a major learning task for English learners, who, of course, have a number of concepts for which they do not have English words.

Learning New Words Representing New Concepts

Another word-learning task students face, and a very demanding one, is learning to read words that are in neither their oral nor their reading vocabularies and for which they do not have an available concept. Learning the full meanings of such words as *equation, impeach,* and *mammal* is likely to require most elementary students to develop new concepts. All students continue to learn words of this sort throughout their years in school and beyond. Once again, learning new concepts will be particularly important for second-language learners. Also, students whose backgrounds differ from that of the majority culture will have internalized a set of concepts that is at least somewhat different than the set internalized by students in the majority culture. Thus, words that represent known concepts for some groups of students will represent unknown concepts for other groups.

Learning New Meanings for Known Words

Still another word-learning task is learning new meanings for words that students already know with one meaning. Many words have multiple meanings, and thus students frequently encounter words that look familiar but are used with a meaning different from the one they know. Students will encounter such words throughout the elementary grades and beyond. Teaching these words occupies a special place in content areas such as science and social studies because words often have different and important meanings that are critical to comprehension in particular content areas. The meaning of *product* in mathematics and that of *legend* in geography or history are just two examples of such words.

Clarifying and Enriching the Meanings of Known Words

The meanings students originally attach to words are often imprecise and only become fully specified over time; thus, another word-learning task is that of clarifying and enriching the meanings of already-known words. For example, at some point students might not recognize any difference between *brief* and *concise* or not know what distinguishes a *cabin* from a *shed*. Although students will expand and enrich the meanings of the words they know as they repeatedly meet them in new and slightly different contexts, some more direct approaches to expanding and enriching word meanings are warranted.

Moving Words into Students' Expressive Vocabularies

Still another word-learning task is that of moving words from students' receptive vocabularies to their productive vocabularies, that is, moving words from students' listening and reading vocabularies to their speaking and writing vocabularies. Third graders, for example, might know the meaning of the word *fortunate* when they hear it or read it yet never use the word themselves, and sixth graders might know the word *ignite* but not use it. Most people actively use only a small percentage of the words they know. Assisting students in actively using the words they know will make them better and more precise communicators.

SUMMING UP

Each of the factors I have discussed in this chapter is important to consider as we plan vocabulary instruction and as we teach individual words. For example, we need to know if we are teaching listening vocabulary or reading vocabulary because instruction for these two types of vocabulary will vary. We need to know how many words students must learn so we can figure out how much time we can afford to spend on individual words. We need to know what depth of word knowledge we are trying to build because building deeper levels of word knowledge will require more time. And we need to know what learning tasks students face in learning a word or group of words because different sorts of instruction are appropriate for different learning tasks.

CHAPTER 3

Common Considerations for Vocabulary Instruction

In Chapters 4, 5, and 6, I discuss specific procedures for building students' oral vocabularies, providing in-depth instruction, and providing introductory instruction. In this chapter, I describe instructional considerations for all types of vocabulary instruction. These include the frequency distribution of English words, selecting vocabulary to teach, principles of effective vocabulary instruction, the importance of student-friendly definitions, and special considerations for English learners.

THE FREQUENCY DISTRIBUTION OF ENGLISH WORDS

In Chapter 2, I noted that the English language consists of more than 180,000 words, that the average high school senior has a vocabulary of something like 50,000 words, and that the average eighth grader has a vocabulary of something like 35,000 words. The main point to understand from these facts is that there are a huge number of words you might teach. Another fact about the English lexicon that is critical to consider as we plan vocabulary instruction is that the lexicon consists of a small number of very frequent words, a somewhat larger number of somewhat frequent words, and a very large number of infrequent words. The 100 most frequent words account for about 50% of the words in a typical text. The 1,000 most frequent words account for about 70% of the words in a typical text. And the 5,000 most frequent words account for about 80% of the words in a typical text (Hiebert, 2005). If a student does not know these very frequent words, she will be repeatedly stumbling over the words in anything other than a book with severely controlled vocabulary, something like a beginning basal or a high-interest easy-reading book.

Further appreciation of the importance of frequent words can be gained from considering an actual text and looking at the frequent words it contains, something I do in Figure 3.1. The figure makes use of the work of Hiebert (2005), who recently developed a *Word Zones*™ list of approximately 4,000 word families (base words and their common inflected forms) using data from Zeno, Ivens, Millard, and Duvvuri's *The Educator's Word Frequency Guide* (1995), the most recent large-scale frequency count of American English. Hiebert divided the 4,000 words into four "zones": the first 300 most frequent words, the next 500 words, the next 1,200 words, and the final 2,000 words. The value of knowing these frequent words is shown in the four panels of Figure 3.1. The figure shows a passage from a biography of Charles Lindberg (Giblin, 1997, p. 3) written for upper-elementary students and the words that would be familiar to students who knew (1) only the 300 words in Zone 1, (2) the 800 words in Zones 1–2, (3) the 2,000 words in Zones 1–3, and (4) the 4,000 words in Zones 1–4.

FIGURE 3.1. Intermediate-Grade Passage Showing What Students Could Read If They Knew 300, 800, 2,000, and 4,000 Words

(1) Knowing only the 300 words in Zone 1, a student could read only the words shown here.

Could it be an _____ ? The year before, _____ had seen one for the first time when his mother took him to a _____ _____ in _____ _____, _____. He had _____, _____, as the _____ _____ a _____ _____ by _____ _____ on the _____ of a _____ that was _____ on the _____. Now _____ an _____ was right here in _____, and about to _____ over his house.
 Not _____ to _____ a thing, _____ _____ the _____ _____ and _____ up the _____ of the house to its _____. From there he had a good _____ of the _____, _____ the _____ place. And in the _____, _____ ever_____, he saw the _____.

(2) Knowing the 800 words in Zones 1 and 2, a student could read the words shown in this version.

Could it be an _____? The year before, _____ had seen one for the first time when his mother took him to a _____ _____ in _____ _____, _____. He had watched, _____, as the _____ gave a _____ _____ by _____ _____ on the _____ of a _____ that was _____ on the ground. Now maybe an _____ was right here in _____, and about to _____ over his house.
 Not _____ to _____ a thing, _____ opened the window and _____ up the _____ of the house to its _____. From there he had a good view of the _____ River, _____ past the _____ place. And in the sky, coming ever _____, he saw the _____.

(3) Knowing the 2,000 words in Zones 1–3, a student could read the words shown in this version.

Could it be an airplane? The year before, Charles had seen one for the first time when his mother took him to a flying _____ in _____, Virginia. He had watched, _____, as the _____ gave a _____ _____ by _____ oranges on the _____ of a _____ that was _____ on the ground. Now maybe an airplane was right here in _____, and about to fly over his house. Not _____ to _____a thing, Charles opened the window and climbed up the _____ roof of the house to its _____. From there he had a good view of the _____ River, _____ past the _____ place. And in the sky, coming ever closer, he saw the plane.

FIGURE 3.1. *Continued*

---

(4) Knowing the 4,000 words Zones 1–4, a student would be able to read everything in the version below that is not underlined.

> Could it be an airplane? The year before, Charles had seen one for the first time when his mother took him to a flying <u>exhibition</u> in Fort <u>Myer</u>, Virginia. He had watched, <u>enthralled</u>, as the pilot gave a bombing <u>demonstration</u> by dropping oranges on the outline of a battleship that was traced on the ground. Now maybe an airplane was right here in Minnesota, and about to fly over his house.
>
> Not wanting to miss a thing, Charles opened the window and climbed up the sloping roof of the house to its peak. From there he had a good view of the Mississippi River, flowing <u>languidly</u> past the <u>Lindbergh</u> place. And in the sky, coming ever closer, he saw the plane. (Giblin, 1997, p. 3)

As can be seen, knowing as few as 300 words, a student would be able to read over half the words in the passage. However, this is not nearly enough to lead to comprehension. Knowing as few as 800 words, the student would be able to read well over half the words in the passage but still not enough to lead to comprehension. Knowing 2,000 words, the student would be able to read about 80% of the words but would still be unable to understand the passage. However, with knowledge of the most frequent 4,000 words, the student would know over 90% of the words in the passage, could begin to comprehend it, could make some reasonable inferences about the words she did not know, or could be taught the meanings of the unknown words. Thus, knowing these very frequent words is crucial, and not knowing them is very debilitating.

Now consider the words beyond these 4,000 most frequent ones. Remember there are more than 180,000 of them. What these words have in common is that they are quite infrequent. Here are some examples: *Junk*, roughly the 5,000th most frequent word, occurs 11 times per million running words. *Dodge*, roughly the 10,000th most frequent, occurs 3 times per million running words. And *jilted*, roughly the 100,000th most frequent, occurs something like 1 time per 5 million running words (Zeno et al., 1995). If we assume that a typical fifth grader might read something like 1 million words a year (a reasonable estimate according to Nagy, Herman, & Anderson, 1985), then that fifth grader is likely to encounter *junk* only

11 times during the year, *dodge* only 3 times, and *jilted* not at all. This means that we need to select words to teach very carefully and typically on the basis of criteria that go beyond simply considering their overall frequency.

SELECTING VOCABULARY TO TEACH

Here, I recommend a process in which you first get some idea of which words are likely to be unknown to your students and then follow several criteria for selecting the specific words you will teach. As recent scholarship makes clear, this is a task that deserves serious attention (see Hiebert & Lubliner, in press; Nagy & Hiebert, 2007).

Identifying Unknown Words

Three sources can be useful for identifying words to teach— word lists, the selections students are reading or listening to, and students themselves.

Word Lists. Word lists are a good starting point in identifying words to teach. They can tell you which words are frequent and which are infrequent. They can also tell you something about which words students are likely to know and which words are important to know. The list of very frequent words I am currently using is one that two colleagues and I (Graves, Sales, & Ruda, 2008) derived from Hiebert's *Word Zones*™ list. Our list, which we call *The First 4,000 Words*, is simply a list of the roughly 4,000 most frequent word families listed in order of their frequency. It is available online at thefirst4000words.com. Many students come to school with all of these words already in their oral vocabularies and will learn to read them over the first several years of school. Other students, however, do not come to school with all of these words in their oral vocabularies and will need help in getting them into both their oral vocabularies and their reading vocabularies. As the examples in Figure 3.1 clearly show, if students do not know these words, they are a definite priority.

Two additional lists of relatively frequent words have recently been developed by Biemiller and will be published in an upcoming book titled *Words Worth Teaching* (in press). Based on some previous testing of students' word knowledge, testing Biemiller and his colleagues did, and Biemiller and his colleagues' intuition based on the work they have done, Biemiller has developed these lists of words potentially worth teaching. These are less frequent than those in *The First 4,000 Words* but still fairly frequent and definitely words students need to learn. The first list, "Words Worth Teaching in Kindergarten Through Grade 2," consists of about 2,000 words. The second, "Words Worth Teaching in Grades Three–Six," and consists of about 4,000 words.

The final list I suggest you consider is Dale and O'Rourke's *The Living Word Vocabulary* (1981). This book presents the results of vocabulary tests administered to students in grades 4, 6, 8, 10, 12, 13, and 16. In all, the tests included about 43,000 items testing about 30,000 words, with several meanings of many of the words being tested. Each item on the test was administered to students at various grade levels until the grade level at which between 67% and 84% of the students tested correctly identified the meaning being tested. The book presents the word tested, the meaning tested, the grade level at which between 67% and 84% of the students knew the particular word-meaning combination, and the exact percentage of students at that grade level who correctly answered the item. The entry for *folly*, which was tested with a single meaning, and the entry for *humble*, which was tested with four meanings, are shown in Figure 3.2.

As can be seen, the test indicates that 67% of the eighth-grade students tested knew the word *folly* with the meaning "foolish act." Each of the entries for *humble* provides similar information. Thus, *The Living Word Vocabulary* provides information you need as you consider teaching a word. That is, it answers the question, "What percent of my students are likely to know this word with this meaning?" Moreover, research (Biemiller, 2004; Graves & Gebhart, 1982) has shown that the predictions are quite accurate. Of course, looking up every word you consider teaching in *The Living Word Vocabulary* is not feasible. However, the book is very valuable for getting a feel for what sorts of words students at various grade levels are likely to know. By identifying some words, predicting the percentage of students in your class likely to know them, and then checking your perceptions against the data in *The Living Word Vocabulary*, you can begin to develop a real feeling for the sorts of words that students of various ages do and do not know. Unfortunately, *The Living Word*

FIGURE 3.2. Sample Entries from The Living Word Vocabulary

Grade	Score	Word	Meaning
8	67%	folly	foolish act
6	76%	humble	modest
8	78%	humble	to make ashamed
8	69%	humble	not proud
12	77%	humble	not rich

Source: Dale & O'Rourke, 1981

Vocabulary is currently available only from libraries, but I believe it is informative enough to be worth searching out.

The Selections Students Are Reading. The second source useful for identifying words that you might teach—and the source that you will use the vast majority of the time—is the selections students are reading or listening to. As I have noted, English includes a small number of frequent words and a very large number of infrequent words. Once students acquire a basic vocabulary of several thousand words, the number of different words you might teach is so large that using word lists to identify words to teach becomes problematic. At this point, using your best judgment to select vocabulary from the material students are reading and listening to becomes the most appropriate approach to take.

The Students Themselves. The third source of information about what words to teach is the students themselves. As a way of sharpening your perceptions of which words your students do and do not know, you can identify words in upcoming selections that you think will be difficult, build multiple-choice or matching tests on these words, and test students to find out whether or not the words are difficult. Of course, constructing such tests is time consuming and certainly not something to be done for every selection. However, after several experiences of identifying words that you think will be difficult and then checking students' performance against your expectations, your general perceptions of which words are and are not likely to cause your students problems will become increasingly accurate.

In addition to testing students on potentially difficult words using multiple-choice or matching tests, you can take the opportunity to occasionally ask students which words they know. One easy way to do this is to list potentially difficult words on the board and have students raise their hands if they don't know a word. This approach is quick, easy, and risk free for students; it also gives students some responsibility for their word learning. Moreover, research (White, Slater, & Graves, 1989) indicates that students can be quite accurate in identifying words that they do and do not know.

Selecting Specific Words to Teach

As I just noted, once students have acquired a basic vocabulary, most of the words you teach should be selected from the material they are reading. Unfortunately, many reading selections will contain more difficult vocabulary than you have time to teach. Thus, once you have identified potentially difficult vocabulary in a selection students are going to read, there is still the matter of deciding just which ones you will teach. The answers to five questions should be helpful:

- *Is understanding the word important to understanding the selection in which it appears?* If the answer is "yes," the word is a good candidate for instruction. If the answer is "no," then other words are probably more important to teach.
- *Does this word represent a specific concept students definitely need to know?* If it does, then that is a very good reason to teach it. If it does not, then it may still be worth teaching for other reasons.
- *Are students able to use context or structural-analysis skills to discover the word's meaning?* If they can use these skills, then they should be allowed to practice them. Doing so will both help them hone these skills and reduce the number of words you need to teach.
- *Can working with this word be useful in furthering students' context, structural-analysis, or dictionary skills?* If the answer here is "yes," then your working with the word can serve two purposes: It can aid students in learning the word, and it can help them acquire a strategy they can use in learning other words. You might, for example, decide to

teach the word *regenerate* because students need to master the prefix *re-*.

*   *How useful is this word outside of the reading selection currently being taught?* The more frequently a word appears in material students read, the more important it is for them to know the word. Additionally, the more frequent a word is, the greater the chances that students will retain the word once you teach it.

As a comment on these five questions, I need to add that they are not independent. In fact, the answer to one question may suggest that a word should be taught, while the answer to another suggests that it should not. Moreover, authorities differ on which criterion should receive precedence. Beck, McKeown, and Kucan (2002, 2008), for example, have suggested that precedence should be given to what they call Tier 2 words. Tier 2 words are words that are used by mature language users, that students are likely to encounter in the texts they read in upcoming years, and that are used across domains—for example, in English, history, and science—and not just in a single domain such as health or music. Tier 2 words are certainly important, but in my judgment, teaching the words that are most important for understanding a particular selection will usually be the foremost consideration.

PRINCIPLES OF EFFECTIVE VOCABULARY INSTRUCTION

We know a tremendous amount about how to teach individual words—how to create really strong instruction. The following set of principles come from my own thinking and that of many other vocabulary authorities, including Stahl and Fairbanks (1986), Herman and Dole (1988), Nagy (1988, 2005), Stahl (1998), Beck and her colleagues (2002, 2008), Biemiller (2004), and Stahl and Nagy (2006). Unfortunately, powerful vocabulary instruction comes at a real cost. It takes time. This is a factor I will consider after listing the principles.

*   *Include both definitional and contextual information.* That is, give students both a definition of the word being taught and the word in context.

- *Involve students in active and deep processing of the word.* Engage students in activities that lead them to consider the word's meaning, relate that meaning to information stored in memory, and work with the word in creative ways. Such activities might include putting the definition of a new word into their own words, giving examples and nonexamples of situations in which the word can be used, examining ways in which the new word relates to them personally, and recognizing similarities and differences between the new word and words they already know.
- *Provide students with multiple exposures to the word.* You might, for example, define the word, use it in a sentence, ask students to use it in a sentence, involve students in recognizing appropriate and not-so-appropriate uses of the word, and play games involving the word.
- *Review, rehearse, and remind students about the word in various contexts over time.* If you teach a word before students read a selection, it is generally a good idea to at least briefly review it after they read. Then, throughout the weeks and months following initial instruction, look for and point out other occurrences of the word, ask students to look for and point out other occurrences, and occasionally have a brief review of some of the words taught.
- *Involve students in discussions of the word's meaning.* Discussion is one method of actively processing word meanings, it gives students the opportunity to hear and use the word in a variety of context, and it enables students to learn from each other.
- *Spend a significant amount of time on the word, involving students in actively grappling with the word's meaning.* With word learning, as with almost all learning, time on task is crucial. The more time you spend on a word, the better the chance that students will build rich and deep meanings for it.

These are sound principles, but each of them should be prefaced with the phrase "for the strongest possible results." As I said at the beginning of this section, there is a definite cost of teaching in a way that achieves the strongest possible results. Doing so takes time. Because there are many more words that could be taught than you can possibly teach and because you have many things to do other than teach words, your time is definitely limited. Often, it will be necessary to teach words in ways that do not consume large amounts of time and do not in fact produce the strongest possible results. In these cases, think of your initial instruction on a word as just that—introductory instruction, an initial experience that starts students on the long road to learning full and rich meanings for the word.

THE IMPORTANCE OF STUDENT-FRIENDLY DEFINITIONS

Student-friendly definitions are carefully crafted definitions deliberately designed to be understandable by young learners. Unfortunately, many definitions in traditional dictionaries are not very useful to children. Student-friendly definitions should use words simpler than the word being defined, use syntax children can easily process, avoid circularity, and leave the learner with a meaning she can grasp. Figure 3.3 shows some traditional definitions and some student friendly ones.

Although many dictionaries do not use student friendly definitions, some do. Two particularly useful sources of student friendly definitions are the *Collins COBUILD New Student's Dictionary* (2005) and the *Longman Study Dictionary of American English* (2006).

FIGURE 3.3. Traditional and Student-Friendly Definitions

TRADITIONAL DEFINITIONS

> **dazzling** Bright enough to deprive someone of sight temporarily. (*Microsoft Word 2004 for Mac*)
> **climate** The prevailing weather conditions of a particular region. (*American Heritage Dictionary*, 2001)
> **contagious** Transmissible by direct or indirect contact; communicable. (*American Heritage Dictionary*, 2001)

STUDENT-FRIENDLY DEFINITIONS

> **dazzling** If something is dazzling, that means that it's so bright that you can hardly look at it. (Beck et al., 2002, p. 55)
> **climate** Climate is the normal weather of a place.
> **contagious** A contagious disease can be caught by touching people or things inflected with it, or sometimes by just getting close to them.

SPECIAL CONSIDERATION FOR ENGLISH LEARNERS

As reviews by Gersten and Baker (2000), Slavin and Cheung (2003), Cummins (2003), August and Shanahan (2006), and August and Snow (2007) make clear, instructional approaches that are effective with native English speakers are likely to be effective with English learners. Nevertheless, there are important considerations to take into account when working with students for whom English is not their first language. The following considerations are taken from the above reviews, from my own reading of the literature, and most importantly from extremely cogent and useful reviews by Goldenberg (2008, in press). In listing these considerations, I include three overarching generalizations about instruction for English learners, some accommodations you can use in any teaching, and some accommodations to use when teaching individual words.

Three Generalizations

- Teaching students to read in their first language promotes higher levels of reading achievement in English. (It should be noted that while the gains produced by beginning with students' first language are very reliable, they are not large.)
- What we know about good instruction and curriculum in general holds true for English learners as well. For example, using consistent classroom management routines is always good practice.
- English learners require instructional accommodations when instructed in English. For example, they often need more time to complete tasks.

General Accommodations

- Make motivation a prime concern.
- Use predictable and consistent classroom management routines.
- Provide additional time and opportunities for practice. When learning is a challenge, having a little extra time can make a big difference.
- Use graphic organizers that make content and concept relationships visually explicit and not totally dependent on language.

- Provide redundant information in nonverbal forms. Whenever possible, key information should be in both verbal and nonverbal forms.
- Scaffold students' reading of difficult texts by providing them with appropriate prereading, during-reading, and post reading activities. *Scaffolding Reading Experience for English Language Learners* (Fitzgerald & Graves, 2004) describes a comprehensive plan for providing English learners with support for the texts they read.
- Help students organize and consolidate text knowledge. Frequent reviews and summaries are key.
- Provide frequent opportunities for interaction with teachers and peers. I particularly recommend pairing English learners with native English-speaking buddies.
- Adjust your speaking rate, the complexity of the sentences you use, and the language expectations you have for English learners.

Accommodations When Teaching Individual Words

- English learners may have considerably smaller English vocabularies than native English speakers. More words will need to be taught, and some of these may be more basic words.
- English learners may need more instruction in oral vocabulary as well as in reading vocabulary.
- More words are likely to represent new concepts, not merely new labels. This means that methods specifically designed to teach concepts will be needed.
- Identifying and teaching potentially difficult vocabulary before students read a selection is likely to be particularly important.
- English learners are likely to profit from stronger initial instruction, multiple exposures, and multiple contexts.
- Rhymes, poems, and games can be particularly useful and provide some fun during what may sometimes be challenging days at school.
- Pictures, demonstrations, concrete objects, and video are likely to be both needed and effective.

SUMMING UP

In this chapter, I have done five things. First, I described the frequency distribution of English words. One point here is that there is a relatively small number of very frequent words and it is vital that students know them. The other is that most English words are infrequent and you will need to carefully select those you take the time to teach. Second, I discussed selecting vocabulary to teach. In doing so, word lists, the selections students are reading, and the students themselves can be used as starting points. Then you are going to need to winnow down the likely lengthy list of words you might teach to a more manageable number. Third, I identified principles of effective vocabulary instruction. We know what sorts of instruction produces powerful results, but we also know that methods that produce powerful results are time consuming. The key is to know when to use more time-consuming methods and when to use less time-consuming methods. Fourth, I discussed student-friendly definitions, the kinds of definitions that students can really learn from. Finally, I suggested special considerations for English learners and a variety of accommodations you can make to help them succeed.

CHAPTER 4

Building Students' Oral Vocabularies

Because reading occupies center stage in the elementary grades, when we think of teaching vocabulary, we immediately think of teaching reading vocabulary. However, it is important that students continually build both their oral vocabularies and their reading vocabularies. Doing so is, of course, important for all students, but it is particularly important for students who arrive at school with small oral vocabularies—a group that includes many English learners. In this chapter, I first discuss techniques for building all students' oral vocabularies and then a technique that has proven to be particularly useful for students who arrive at school with small oral vocabularies.

APPROACHES FOR ALL STUDENTS

Several approaches to increasing all students' oral vocabularies are particularly effective. These include reading aloud to children, using some sophisticated vocabulary in talking to students, complementing and encouraging students when they use words adroitly, and discussing sophisticated topics that invite and even require sophisticated vocabulary. I realize that you already do some of these things, but you may want to make them even more deliberate and more frequent activities in your classroom.

Reading Aloud to Children

As Stahl and Stahl (2004) have pointed out and as the data in Figure 4.1 make clear, books are "where the words are." Children's books contain many more challenging words than children's TV shows, adult TV shows, or the conversations of college graduates (Hayes & Ahrens, 1988). Books are, therefore, a great source of new words.

Reading aloud to children is very frequently recommended, very widely recommended, and very strongly recommended. For example, in *Becoming a Nation of Readers* (Anderson, Hiebert, Scott, & Wilkinson, 1985), one of the most powerful policy statements on reading education ever produced, the authors concluded that "the single most important activity for building knowledge required for eventual success in reading is reading aloud to children." Reading aloud has the potential to introduce children to the joy of reading; build background knowledge; build vocabulary; and familiarize children with text structures, concepts about print, and the distinctive character of written language (Teale, 2003). Moreover, if combined with appropriate prereading, during-reading, and post-reading activities, reading aloud to children can have a positive effect on their comprehension (Morrow & Brittain, 2003). Clearly, reading aloud is an important activity. At the same time, it is neither a panacea nor a magic pill that can take the place of other important literacy activities.

Reading aloud is just one of a number of activities important to building students' vocabularies and reading competence more generally. It is, however, an activity I strongly recommend. Fortunately, there are some simple guidelines for making each read-

FIGURE 4.1. Frequency of Rare Words in Various Sources

I. Printed texts	Rare Words per 1,000
Abstracts of scientific articles	128.0
Newspapers	68.3
Popular magazines	65.7
Adult books	52.7
Children's books	30.9
Preschool books	16.3
II. Television texts	
Prime-time adult shows	22.7
Prime-time children's shows	20.2
Mr. Rogers and Sesame Street	2.0
III. Adult speech	
Expert witness testimony	28.4
College graduates' talk to friends/spouses	17.3

Source: Adapted from Hayes & Ahrens, 1988.

aloud experience just as effective and engaging as possible. Based of over two decades of studying reading aloud, Teale (2003) makes the following very useful recommendations, which I have abbreviated somewhat here:

- Scaffold students' listening experiences. Provide them with pre-, during-, and post-reading activities that ensure their success (see Graves & Graves, 2003). Encourage children to use their background knowledge in meaningful ways when approaching the book.
- Ask questions that invite reactions that keep children engaged in the book.
- Read in a lively, engaging way.
- Encourage children to predict during the reading.
- Focus on important text ideas.

- Talk about a few of the words or phrases in the book in ways that build children's vocabulary knowledge. (modified from pp. 131–132)

Using Sophisticated Vocabulary Yourself

In promoting students' word learning through listening, another powerful tool you have available is the vocabulary you use in the classroom. Whether you teach kindergarten, grade 8, or any grade in between, it is worthwhile making a deliberate effort to include some new and somewhat challenging words in your interactions with students. By "new and somewhat challenging words," I generally mean what Beck, McKeown, and Kucan (2002, 2008) identify as "Tier 2 words." As noted in Chapter 3, Tier 2 words are those that are used by mature language users, that are used in various subject areas, and that students are likely to encounter in the texts they read in upcoming years. Of course, the Tier 2 words you want to introduce to students differ from one grade level to another. Note that at this point I am not talking about teaching these words, I am simply talking about using somewhat challenging words from time to time, sometimes pausing to explain their meanings but sometimes just letting students hear them. For example, you might tell a group of first graders that, while it is important to be polite in class, there is no reason to be *timid*. Or you might tell a group of seventh graders who have just come in from lunch and brought with them their cafeteria conversations that the *cacophony* they imported from lunch will not be needed in class. The goal is to expose students to some new and challenging words and to pique their interest in such words.

Complimenting and Encouraging Students' Use of Adept Word Choices

In addition to using some sophisticated vocabulary yourself, you can take the opportunity to compliment students when they use sophisticated words, to discuss the importance of the words they use, and to encourage them to make adept word choices. Doing this is a small thing that doesn't take much time or effort on your part, but it can pay big dividends. We need to sell students on the importance of words and kindle their interest in building their vocabularies. Thus, for example, if during share-and-tell time a second grader announces that his family had to stop talking during breakfast because of the *thunderous* noise of a jet flying overhead, give him a thumbs-up and remark on what how well the word *thunderous* captured the experience. Similarly, if a fifth grader giving a report on healthy eating habits notes that vegetarian dishes can be *delectable*, let him know that *delectable* is a great word. Or if an eighth grader concludes his essay on popular comedians by noting that Robin Williams is a true *extrovert*, you might note that you agree, as well as saying he has chosen the perfect word to describe Williams.

Discussing Topics That Invite Sophisticated Vocabulary

Discussion is still another way to promote word learning, but casual discussions probably will not accomplish much. The key to having discussions that will prompt students to use more sophisticated vocabulary is to give them meaty and somewhat academic topics to talk about. As shown in Figure 4.1, casual conversations, even casual conversations among college graduates, do not include a lot of sophisticated vocabulary. If students are going to use sophisticated words, they need to discuss sophisticated ideas. This means talking about academic topics that students have some familiarity with—topics they are reading about, investigating in the library and on the Internet, and probably writing about. Such discussions might focus on science topics such as the ecology of freshwater lakes, social studies topics such as barriers to ordinary people running for public office, and literary topics such as the motivations that prompt a character's actions. One good source of meaty discussion topics is the literature on teaching for understanding, for example, Wiggins and McTighe's (2005) *Understanding by Design* or Wiske's (1998) *Teaching for Understanding*.

AN APPROACH FOR STUDENTS WITH SMALL VOCABULARIES

The approaches I have discussed thus far are for all children, but some children need more direct assistance in building oral vocabulary. Over the past 30 year, there have been a number of naturalistic studies of mothers reading to their preschool children. And over the past decade or so, there have been a number of experimental studies in which researchers, teachers, parents, and aides used specific procedures in reading to children with the goal of building their oral vocabularies, comprehension, and language skills more generally. Here, I call both the informal procedures mothers use and the more formal ones used in school "shared book reading." The findings of studies on both types of shared book reading are highly consistent and serve to highlight the characteristics of effective approaches to building oral vocabulary in this way. Below, I discuss these characteristics and give some examples of them, drawing heavily on the work of De Temple and Snow (2003) as well as my own synthesis of the literature.

Commonalities of Shared Book Reading

Various types of shared book reading have a good deal in common. Here I list those commonalities. After that, I discuss two specific types of shared book reading: Dialogic Reading and Words in Context.

Effective shared book reading is interactive. That is, both the reader and the children play active roles. The reader frequently pauses, prompts children to respond, and follows up those responses with answers and perhaps more prompts. Children respond to the prompts or questions, elaborate in some of their responses, and perhaps ask questions of their own. Additionally, the interactions are frequently supportive and instructive (Weizman & Snow, 2001). In other words, the reader scaffolds children's efforts to understand the words and the text, as illustrated in the following excerpt of a 5-year-old child and his mother reading Jill Murphy's *What Next, Baby Bear!*

> *Child*: I want to have . . . what are those? Those are those are little little um volcanoes.
> *Mother*: Little *volcanoes*. Well yeah. Kind of. They're *craters*.
> *Child*: Craters?
> *Mother*: Yeah.
> *Child*: And the first comes out of it?
> *Mother*: No. They just look like *volcanoes* but they're not.
> *Child*: Yeah, they're on the moon.
> *Mother*: Yeah. (Quoted in De Temple & Snow, 2003, p. 27.)

Effective shared book reading involves reading the book several times. This allows the children and the reader to revisit the same topic and the same words several times, and it allows the children to begin actively using some of the words they have heard and perhaps had explained in previous readings.

Effective shared book reading directly focuses children's attention on a relatively small number of words. In some cases, the word work comes during the first reading, in some cases during subsequent readings, and in some cases after the book has been read.

Effective shared book reading requires the adult readers to read fluently. Skilled adult readers effectively engage children with their animated and lively reading style.

Effective shared book reading requires carefully selected books. The books need to be interesting and enjoyable for children, and they need to stretch children's thinking a bit. Of course, the books also need to include some challenging words that are worth studying and will enhance children's vocabularies.

Having considered the general characteristics of effective approaches to building vocabulary through oral reading, I turn now to describing two programs that have been shown to be effective and that can be used as models for a program in your school—Whitehurst's *Dialogic Reading* and Biemiller's *Words in Context* (a name I have given the approach). Other approaches you may want to consider include Beck and McKeown's (2001, 2007), *Text Talk,* Juel and Deffes (2004) *Anchored Instruction,* and Silverman's (2007) *Analytic Instruction.*

Dialogic Reading

Dialogic Reading (Whitehurst et al., 1988; Whitehurst et al., 1994; Zevenbergen & Whitehurst, 2003) is a one-to-one technique of shared book reading technique with picture books designed for preschoolers. It can be used by teachers, teacher aides, other caregivers, and parents to foster vocabulary development and language development more generally. Like other techniques of shared book reading, Dialogic Reading begins with the understanding that there are more and less effective ways to orally share books with children and that a carefully designed procedure can maximize the effectiveness of oral reading. The procedure is "based on the theory that practice in using language, feedback regarding language, and appropriately scaffolded adult-child interactions in the context of picture book reading all facilitate young children's language development" (Zevenbergen & Whitehurst, 2003). Two sets of procedures have been developed, one for 2- to 3-year-olds and one for 4- to 5-year-olds. Both procedures encourage the child to become the teller of the story over time, prompt the child by using questions, expand the child's vocabularies by highlighting words that are likely to be new to the child, and praise the child for her efforts in telling the story and labeling objects depicted in the book. Additionally, consistent with Vygotsky's (1978) principle of the zone of proximal development, over time the adult continually nudges the child toward more sophisticated language and thinking than she would be likely to use on her own.

The Dialogic Reading procedure for 4- to 5-year-olds recommends that adult readers elicit children's responses using the five types of prompts shown below:

Prompts Used with Dialogic Reading

- Completion prompts. Fill-in-the-blank questions (e.g., "When we went into the car, we all put on our _____")
- Recall prompts. Questions that require the child to remember aspects of the book (e.g., "Can you remember some of the things that Sticky-beak did at school?")
- Open-ended prompts. Statements that encourage the child to respond to the book in his or her terms (e.g., "Now it's your turn to tell about this page.")
- Wh-prompts. What, where, and why questions (e.g., "What is this called?" "Why did Peter stay home from school?")
- Distancing prompts. Questions that require the child to relate the content of the book to aspects of life outside of school (e.g., "Did we ever go to a parade like Susan did?") (Zevenbergen & Whitehurst, 2003, p. 180)

The approach also includes the four procedures listed below.

Procedures Used with Dialogic Reading

- Prompt. Ask the child to label objects in the pictures and talk about the story (e.g., pointing to a picture, "What do you call this?" "Why do you think the puppy looks sad?")
- Evaluate. Praise the child's correct answers and offer alternate labels or correct answers for incorrect responses (e.g., "Very good. That is a puppy." "No, that's not a kitten, it's a puppy.")
- Expand. Repeat what the child said and add information not in the child's response (e.g., "Yes, the puppy does look sad. I think that's because he doesn't have a home. Do you think that would make him sad?")
- Repeat. Guide the child to repeat the expanded response (e.g., "Can you tell me why the puppy might look sad?")

Each instance of Dialogic Reading is, of course, somewhat different, but the following parent–child Dialogic Reading of Ezra Jack Keats's *The Snowy Day* is a good example:

Parent: "The Snowy Day." What's he doing here?
Child: Sliding.
Parent: Yeah. He's sliding down a hill. Can you say that?
Child: He's sliding down a hill.
Parent: Good. "One winter morning Peter woke up and looked out the window. Snow had fallen during the night. It covered everything as far as he could see." What does he see outside his window?
Child: Snow.
Parent: That's right. There's lots of snow outside.
Child: Yeah.
Parent: "After breakfast he put on his snowsuit and ran outside. The snow was piled up very high along the street to make a path for walking." Your turn. What's happening on this page?
Child: He is making steps in the snow.
Parent: That's right. He's making footprints.
Child: Footprints.
Parent: Do you remember when we played outside in the snow?

Child: Yeah. And we made snowballs.

Parent: You remember. We made a lot of snowballs. I remember that you made footprints all around the yard too.

Child: Yeah.

Parent: "Then he dragged his feet s-l-o-w-l-y to make tracks. And he found something sticking out of the snow that made a new track." What do you think it was that made a new track?

Child: A dog?

Parent: Well, it looks like it might be something else that makes the track. Let's see what it is next. "It was a _____ "

Child: Stick.

Parent: Yes. "It was a stick—a stick that was right for making a snow-covered _____

Child: Tree.

Parent: Okay. What happens next?

Child: He got snow on his head.

Parent: That's right. (Zevenbergen & Whitehurst, 2003, pp. 195–196)

There are two videotapes designed to prepare parents and teachers to use Dialogic Reading (*Read Together, Talk Together Parent Video*, 2002; *Read Together, Talk Together Teacher Training Video*, 2002).

Words in Context

Words in Context (Biemiller, 2001, 2003; Biemiller & Boote, 2006) is a technique for shared book reading intended for kindergarten through second-grade children. The procedure includes some very direct instruction, more direct than that provided in some of the other approaches. Also, Words in Context differs from some of the other approaches in that vocabulary development is the sole concern. The procedure is directly motivated by the fact that the vocabularies of disadvantaged children often lag well behind those of their more advantaged peers and that the instruction needed to make up that gap needs to be "early, direct, and sequential" (Biemiller, 2001).

The first step is to select books. The program uses one book per week, and in order to teach the number of words necessary to markedly increase disadvantaged students' vocabularies, the program should be used for at least 1 year and preferably for 3 years.

About 30 books are needed for each year. As it has usually been implemented, the approach uses narratives. Typical of books appropriate for kindergarten are Norman Birdwell's *Clifford at the Circus* and Phoebe Gillman's *Jillian Jiggs*. Typical of those appropriate for grade 1 are Alice Schertle's *Down the Road* and Dayal Khalsa's *Julian*. And typical of those appropriate for grade 2 are Leo Lionni's *Alexander and the Wind-Up Mouse* and Stephanie McLellan's *The Chicken Cat*.

The next step, one that Biemiller (2005, in press) has given very careful attention to, is selecting words. In the past, words were selected based on the teacher's intuition that they are (1) known by some but not all children at the grade level at which you are working and (2) are not rare or obscure words and thus are likely to be useful to children as they progress into the upper elementary grades. However, Biemiller's (in press) recently completed list of 2,000 words appropriate for kindergartners through second graders that I described in Chapter 3 makes selecting words to teach a much less intuitive task. Some samples of words that have been used with the procedure and the percentages of students Biemiller and Boote (2006) reported as knowing the words prior to instruction are shown in Figure 4.2.

Two important characteristics of these words should be noted. First, they are not rare and obscure words. They are words that children are likely to hear, and they are words that they are likely to find in the books they read in the elementary years. Second, they span a range of difficulty. Since this is a whole-class procedure, the goal is to include some words that will be a challenge for most of the children and some that will be a challenge for only some children.

FIGURE 4.2. Sample of Words Used with Words in Context

Kindergarten	First Grade	Second Grade
slip (8%)	snag (4%)	envy (3%)
obey (16%)	chance (11%)	scowl (12%)
coop (22%)	certainly (29%)	glance (26%)
parade (34%)	realize (45%)	restless (40%)
fairy (57%)	pile (72%)	appetite (50%)

Source: Biemiller & Boote, 2006.

Select about 24 words from each book. Students will not remember all the words that are taught, but Biemiller estimates that if this number of words were taught each week over a schoolyear, children might learn 400 words. While such learning will not result in children with the smallest vocabularies catching up with those with larger vocabularies, it is a significant improvement over what they would know without instruction.

The third step is to implement the procedure. Here is what it looks like.

Teaching Procedure for Words in Context

- *Day 1.* Read the book through once, including some comprehension questions after reading it but not interrupting the reading with vocabulary instruction. Experience has shown that children may object to interrupting the first reading of the book with vocabulary instruction.
- *Day 2.* Reread the book, teaching about eight words. When you come to a sentence containing a target word, stop and reread the sentence.

   After rereading the word, give a brief explanation. For example, after reading the sentence "It seemed like a good solution" in a second-grade book, pose the question, "What does *solution* mean?" Then answer your question with something like, "A solution is the answer to a problem." Remember to keep the definitions simple, direct, and focused on the meaning of the word as it is used in the story. At the end of the day's instruction, review the words taught by rereading the sentence in which they appeared and the definition you gave.
- *Days 3 and 4.* Reread the story two more times, teaching about eight new words each time. As on Day 2, briefly define the words as you come to them and review all of them at the end of the reading.
- At the end of the week, review all 24 words taught that week, this time using a new context sentence to provide some variety, but giving the same definition.

Used in this way, the procedure will require about half an hour a day and will, as noted earlier, result in students learning something like 400 words over the course of a year. Of course, if the procedure is used from kindergarten through second grade—and this is Biemiller's goal—an even more significant number of words will be learned.

SUMMING UP

Building students' oral vocabularies is vitally important. It is also something that schools have not given much attention to, at least up until very recently. While building oral vocabulary is particularly important for students who arrive at school with small vocabularies, it is important for all students. We can help all students build their oral vocabularies by reading aloud to children, using some sophisticated vocabulary in talking to students, complimenting and encouraging students when they use words well, and discussing sophisticated topics that invite and even demand sophisticated vocabulary. We can help children who enter school with relatively small vocabularies—including English learners with small English vocabularies—by using shared book reading activities such as Dialogic Reading and Words in Context.

In concluding this chapter, I want to stress that the approaches to increasing the oral vocabularies of all children I described are easily implemented. Unfortunately, this is not the case with shared book reading. Activities like Dialogic Reading and Words in Context require that children most in need of oral vocabulary be identified, that they receive something like 30 minutes of special instruction per day, and that they receive this instruction over a considerable period of time—months and even years. This is difficult and time consuming, and therefore costly; but is it something that children with very small vocabularies desperately need.

CHAPTER 5

Rich and Powerful Instruction

S tudies of teaching rarely lead to certainty. Method A works well with one group of students but then fails with another. Method B appears very effective in one study but turns out to be much weaker than Method C in another. What looked like a great idea a decade ago looks rather silly today. Studies of vocabulary instruction are an exception. As I noted in Chapter 3, we know a tremendous amount about how to create rich and powerful vocabulary instruction. Here are the general principles I listed earlier, reproduced in an abbreviated form:

- Give students a definition of the words being taught, and have them work with the words in context.
- Involve students in active and deep processing of the words.
- Provide students with multiple exposures to the words.
- Review, rehearse, and remind students about the words in various contexts over time.
- Involve students in discussions of the words' meanings.
- Spend a significant amount of time on the words, involving students in actively grappling with the their meanings.

In the remainder of this chapter, I describe 12 rich and powerful techniques for teaching individual words, techniques in keeping with these principles. All of them take significant amounts of time, and with all of them the time you spend will pay off in powerful learning. In general, I have listed the less time consuming and less powerful techniques first and the more time consuming and more powerful ones later. However, all of them are quite powerful and fairly time consuming. Also, some of these techniques differ in terms of their purpose—whether, for example, they teach new labels or new concepts. I'll point out these differences in the descriptions of the individual techniques.

SEMANTIC MAPPING

Semantic Mapping is a tried-and-true method that is described at length in an IRA monograph (Heimlich & Pittelman, 1986) and has been successfully used by teachers for a number of years. Here is the way it is done:

- Put a word representing a central concept on the chalkboard, overhead, or LCD screen.
- Ask students to work in groups listing as many words related to the central concept as they can.
- Write students' words on the chalkboard, overhead, or LCD grouped in broad categories.

- Have students name the categories and perhaps suggest additional ones.
- Discuss with students the central concept, the other words, the categories, and their interrelationships.

Figure 5.1 shows a semantic map for makes of cars, and Figure 5.2 shows a semantic map for the word *trees.*

What is particularly important to recognize about Semantic Mapping is that it is both a vocabulary technique and a comprehension technique. For example, one likely occasion for using Semantic Mapping with the word *trees* is as a review after students have read an informational text on trees. Completing a semantic map after reading a selection gives students a chance to share and solidify what they have learned. Semantic Mapping could also be used for the same purpose after students read a passage on *makes of cars,* but since many students are likely to know quite a bit about makes of cars, in this case the procedure might be used before students read the selection and serve as an advance organizer. In both cases, Semantic Mapping does a good deal more than simply teach the terms; it involves students in working with the overall meaning of the selection.

SEMANTIC FEATURE ANALYSIS

Semantic Feature Analysis is another tried-and-true method, another method described in detail in an IRA monograph (Pittelman, Heimlich, Berglund, & French, 1991), and another method that has been used by many teachers over the years. The central feature of Semantic Feature Analysis is a grid that contains a set of related words on one axis and a list of features that each of the words may or may not have on the other axis. Figure 5.3 shows a completed grid for *dwellings.* Although Semantic Feature Analysis is probably as powerful as Semantic Mapping and requires about the same amount of time, it differs from Semantic Mapping in two important ways. First, it is squarely focused on the meaning of words rather than on the meaning of a selection students are reading. Second, it involves simultaneous consideration of a set of words; in fact, the essence of Semantic Feature Analysis is considering differences, sometimes subtle differences, in the meanings of related words.

FIGURE 5.1. Semantic Map for Makes of Cars

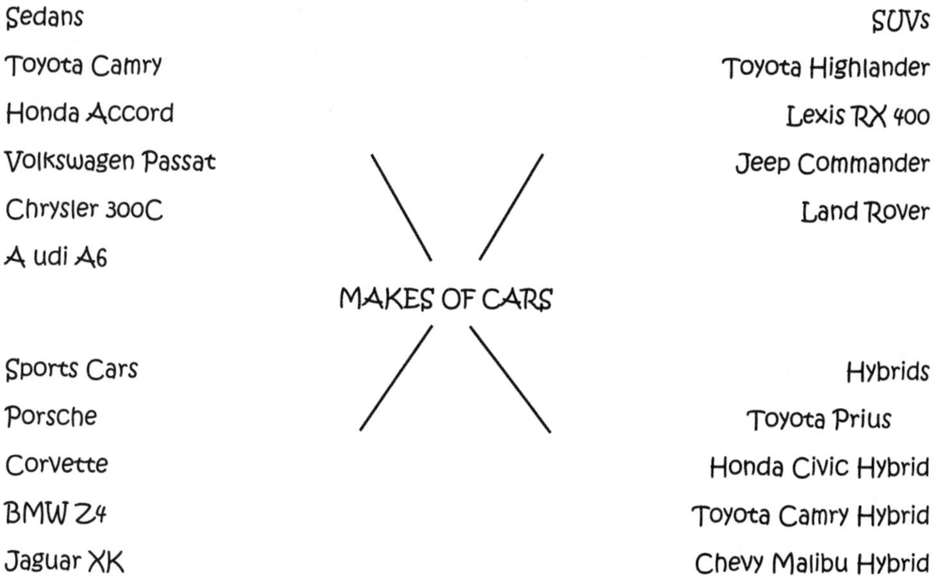

Sedans
Toyota Camry
Honda Accord
Volkswagen Passat
Chrysler 300C
Audi A6

SUVs
Toyota Highlander
Lexis RX 400
Jeep Commander
Land Rover

MAKES OF CARS

Sports Cars
Porsche
Corvette
BMW Z4
Jaguar XK

Hybrids
Toyota Prius
Honda Civic Hybrid
Toyota Camry Hybrid
Chevy Malibu Hybrid

FIGURE 5.2. Semantic Map for Trees

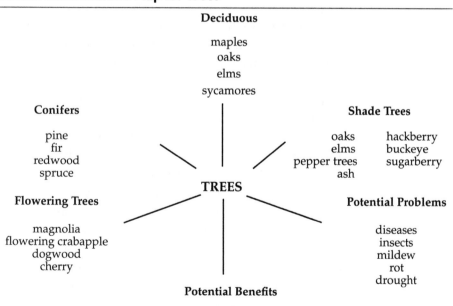

Deciduous
maples
oaks
elms
sycamores

Conifers
pine
fir
redwood
spruce

Shade Trees
oaks   hackberry
elms   buckeye
pepper trees   sugarberry
ash

TREES

Flowering Trees
magnolia
flowering crabapple
dogwood
cherry

Potential Problems
diseases
insects
mildew
rot
drought

Potential Benefits
provide shade   reduces ozone
give off oxygen   are pretty
something to climb   place for tree houses
place for wildlife

FIGURE 5.3. Semantic Feature Analysis Grid for Dwellings

| DWELLINGS | TYPICAL CHARACTERISTICS | | | | | |
	ancient	current	modest	fancy	small	large
cave	+	-	+	-	+	-
pit house	+	-	+	-	+	-
cliff dwelling	+	-	+	-	+	+
hut	+	-	+	-	+	-
castle	+	+	-	+	-	+
shack	-	+	+	-	+	-
cabin	-	+	+	-	+	+
mansion	-	+	-	+	-	+

Here is how it works.

- The first time you work with Semantic Feature Analysis with a particular group of students, you will need to teach them how to use the procedure. In doing so, it is a good idea to present them with a completed grid such as that shown in Figure 5.3 and explain how the pluses and minuses indicate whether or not a particular feature applies to each word.
- As students examine the grid, lead a discussion in which you consider how the features identified in the *dwellings* grid apply to the various words. As in much vocabulary work, discussion is crucial. One thing that is likely to come up as students discuss the *dwellings* grid is that the words *cave, pit house,* and *hut* share the same features. This is likely to lead to further discussion in which students consider whether additional features should be added in order to distinguish among these terms. Clearly they should; these terms are not synonyms. Coming up with distinguishing features is not simple and makes students think. That, of course, is exactly what we want them to do. The important thing that happens in these discussions is that students think closely about the meanings of words and come to distinguish some of the subtle ways in which the English lexicon works.

FIGURE 5.4. Uncompleted Semantic Feature Analysis Grid for Sports

SPORTS	team	individual	profes-sional	amateur	Olympic	not Olympic
football						
basketball						
baseball						
tennis						
golf						
skiing						
bowling						
jogging						

TYPICAL CHARACTERISTICS

- Once students are familiar with the procedure, show them grids with the terms and attributes filled in but without the pluses and minuses, one like that shown in Figure 5.4. Ask them, probably in pairs or small groups, to insert pluses and minuses showing which features apply to which words, to discuss the words and the ways in which their meanings differ in their groups, and then to share their responses with the class.
- Later still, as students become increasingly proficient with the procedure, you can show grids with some terms and some attributes and ask students to add to both the list of related terms and the list of attributes. After this, they can fill in the pluses and minuses and discuss their results.
- Finally, after students are proficient in working with partially completed grids that you supply, they can create their own grids for sets of related words they suggest.

FOUR SQUARES

Four Squares (Schwartz & Raphael, 1985; Stahl & Nagy, 2006) is a straightforward procedure for teaching individual words and the concepts they represent. It is particularly easy to use because it does not require much preparation.

- Begin Four Squares by asking students to fold a blank piece of paper into four parts or simply draw lines to divide the paper into four equal sections. At the same time, put a blank four-square matrix similar to the generic one in Figure 5.5 on the chalkboard, overhead, or LCD screen.
- Have students write the word to be defined in the upper left quadrant. Provide them with a student-friendly definition of the word, but don't have them write it down because they will later be writing their own definitions. Here, I will use the word *buoyant* as an example (see Figure 5.6).
- Ask students for some examples of things that are buoyant and record them in the upper right quadrant. Some possible responses are shown in the upper right quadrant of Figure 5.6. If you get a response that seems incorrect, lead the class toward a more accurate response. You don't want misinformation recorded.
- After several students have had an opportunity to give examples and you have enough examples to illustrate the concept, ask students for some nonexamples, some things that are not buoyant. Record these in the lower right quadrant as shown in Figure 5.6. Again, question any responses that don't seem to work, and record only useful nonexamples.
- Finally, ask students to compose their own definitions of *buoyant* and write these in the lower left quadrant of their individual four-square sheets. Once they have done this, have students share their definitions, and add at least one of them to the class four-square sheet.

Four Squares is a good example of a technique that you can expand on as you choose. You can, for example, solicit more examples and nonexamples, ask students to explain why their examples and nonexamples are good ones, or work with students to make their definitions more precise.

VENN DIAGRAMS

Venn Diagrams (Nagy, 1988) differ from the Four Square approach because with Venn Diagrams you typically investigate the meanings of two words, in the process figuring out which characteristics are exclusive to one word, which are exclusive to the other word,

FIGURE 5.5. Generic Four Squares Grid

The word	*Examples of the concept* example 1 example 2 example 3 example xxx
Definition of the word generated by a student or the class	*Nonexamples of the concept* nonexample 1 nonexample 2 nonexample 3 nonexample xxx

FIGURE 5.6. Four Squares Grid for the Word *Buoyant*

buoyant	boats canoes balloons capped bottles
A thing that is buoyant floats	bricks steel nails marbles

and which are shared. Again, the procedure is simple and straightforward.

- Choose two words with overlapping meanings, such as *short stories* and *essays*, both of which are writing forms.
- Draw an empty Venn Diagram, two overlapping circles, on the chalkboard, overhead, or LCD. A convenient tool for drawing them is available at www.teach-ology.com.
- Discuss the characteristics unique to each word and those common to both of them, and fill in the Venn Diagram accordingly.

FIGURE 5.7. Venn Diagram for *Short Stories* and *Essays*

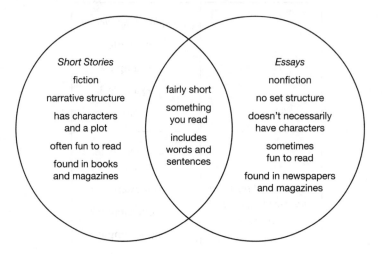

FIGURE 5.8. Venn Diagram for *Canada* and the *United States*

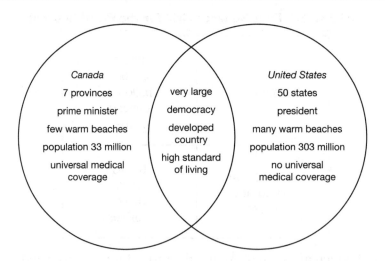

A Venn Diagram for the terms *short stories* and *essays* is shown in Figure 5.7, and one for the terms *Canada* and the *United States* is shown in Figure 5.8. As with any activity, the first time you use Venn Diagrams, you will want to model the procedure, thinking aloud as you complete the diagram and generally doing most of the work. Later, of course, students do more and more of the work, and eventually they can complete Venn Diagrams in pairs or small groups and then share their findings with the class.

VOCABULARY SELF-COLLECTION STRATEGY

The Vocabulary Self-Collection Strategy (Haggard, 1986; Ruddell & Shearer, 2002) differs from the techniques I have described thus far in that it is specifically designed so that students, rather than the teacher, select the words to study. Because of this, it is particularly likely to get students interested and excited about words. Here is how it is typically done:

- Emphasize the importance of vocabulary and the importance of students taking charge of their own learning.
- Ask each student in the class to select one word that he wants to study and thinks is important for the class to learn. Typically, a particular set of words is studied for a week, and often students are allowed to choose their words from any sources: school reading, recreational reading, the Internet, TV, conversations, popular songs, or anyplace else they come across an interesting and important word.
- Tell students to bring in their word, where they found it, what they think it means, and why it is important for the class to know. Also, bring in a word yourself.
- Once words are submitted, use discussion and perhaps the dictionary to clarify their meanings, and have students record the words and definitions in a vocabulary journal.
- During the week, work with the words in various ways using discussion, Semantic Mapping, Semantic Feature Analysis, and other interactive techniques.
- At the end of the week, evaluate students on their ability to explain the words' meanings and to use them in sentences.

While these steps describe the form the Vocabulary Self-Collection technique typically takes, like other instructional techniques, it can be modified to fit you and your class. It can be used for any length of time and need not follow a weekly schedule, and it works very well when the sources of words are limited to the content materials students are currently studying. In fact, my work with the technique has shown it to be particularly valuable for studying content-area vocabulary. Figure 5.9 shows some words brought in by some

FIGURE 5.9. Words Selected by Eighth Graders Using the Vocabulary Self-Collection Strategy

ajar	curriculum	insensate
melancholy	epilepsy	magnetosphere
eureka*	paunch	foreign
flourished	epochs	lustrous
premonition	comprehension*	convergent
conglomerate	persevere	Grenada

*words selected by the teacher

eighth-grade students Ruddell and Shearer (2002) worked with and illustrates the sophisticated words students chose.

POSSIBLE SENTENCES

Possible Sentences (Stahl & Kapinus, 1991) is a prereading procedure that has been shown to be particularly useful with informational text. It teaches a group of words, and it focuses on both vocabulary and comprehension. Here are the steps:

- Choose 6 to 8 words that might cause difficulty for students from an upcoming selection. These should represent key concepts and related words.
- Select an additional 4 to 6 words that are likely to be familiar to students. These familiar words are used to help students generate sentences.
- Put the 10 to 12 words on the board. If some students in the class know the definitions, they can define them. If not, provide student-friendly definitions.
- Ask students to create sentences that use at least two of the words and that are *possible sentences* in the selection they are about to read; that is, ask students to create sentences that could appear in the upcoming selection.
- Put the sentences students create on the board. After that, have them read the selection.
- Once students have finished reading, return to the sentences on the board and discuss whether each of them could be true given the content of the reading selection. Leave sentences that could be true as they are. Have the

class discuss sentences that could not be true and modify them so that they could be true.

Shown in Figure 5.10 are some of the words Stahl and Kapinus selected from a science text they worked with and a few of the possible sentences students might generate with the words. And shown in Figure 5.11 are some words from a social studies chapter I have worked with and a few of the possible sentences students might generate with these words.

FOCUSED DISCUSSION

Focused Discussion (Nagy, 1988) centers students' attention on a key concept, but in discussing that key concept students also work with the meanings of many related words and ideas. In the following example, the key concept is *stereotype*.

- Divide the class into two groups, and assign a recorder for each group.
- Ask one group to brainstorm as many words or phrases

FIGURE 5.10. Difficult Words, Familiar Words, and Possible Sentences from a Science Chapter

Potentially difficult words: *front, barometer, humidity, air mass, air pressure, meteorology*

Familiar words: *clouds, rain, predict*

When a *front* approaches, it is quite likely to *rain*. (could be true)

Most people don't like days with a lot of *humidity* or with a lot of *clouds*. (could be true)

When a *front* approaches, it is very unlikely to *rain*. (could not be true)

FIGURE 5.11. Difficult Words, Familiar Words, and Possible Sentences from a Social Studies Chapter

Potentially difficult words: *woodland people, wickiups, sleeping shelf, tundra, blubber, pasture, herbs*

Familiar words: *forest, winter, hunters, fire, poles*

Woodland people live mostly in the *forest*. (could be true)

Living on the *tundra* is difficult, particularly in the *winter*. (could be true)

Wickiups can easily be constructed without *poles*. (could not be true) as they can that are associated with the word *cities*. Ask the other group to brainstorm words or phrases associated with the phrase *small towns*.

- Have the recorder in each group write down the words and phrases brainstormed.
- Give groups about 3 minutes for brainstorming, and then ask each recorder to read the group's list. Figure 5.12 shows some of the word associations that students might come up with for *cities* and *small towns*. Encourage students to ask questions about the words and to comment on the appropriateness of the words on their lists.
- Introduce the concept *stereotype*, explaining it in terms of oversimplified and formulaic views and attitudes about people, places, and institutions. Ask students whether or not any of the ideas on their lists reflect stereotypes of big cities or small towns and the people who live in them.
- Spend some time discussing stereotypes, noting that people and places do not often fit the stereotyped images, and observing that stereotyping often blinds us to the realities and to recognizing the unique aspects of people, places, and other things.

Focused Discussion is one more good example of the centrality of discussion in much vocabulary instruction.

VOCABULARY VISITS

Vocabulary Visits (Blachowicz & Obrochta 2005, 2007) is a procedure for teaching content vocabulary to primary-grade students. It provides in-depth study of a group of words and at the same time makes vocabulary learning fun and gets students interested and excited about words. The procedure is modeled after field trips that students greatly enjoy and learn from. As is the case with well-run field trips, Vocabulary Visits (1) prepares students for the journey; (2) encourages use of various senses; (3) provides mediation and assistance by an adult; (4) involves exploration, talk, reading, and writing; and (5) includes follow-up activities. Doing all this might take several weeks, so this is really a vocabulary unit. Here is how the procedure unfolds:

FIGURE 5.12. Possible Associations for *Cities* and *Small Towns* While Studying Stereotypes

Cities	Small Towns
noisy	boring
busy	quiet
dangerous	dull
lots to do	not much fun
lots of movies to go to	everybody know you
fun	clean
exciting	slow
dirty	things close early
fast paced	you make good friends
things stay open late	

- Identify a central topic for your grade level and several brief informational books on that topic—for example, skeletons, recycling, or Colonial America. The books should range in difficulty, with each successive book being just a bit more challenging. Scan the books, and select the core vocabulary that you want to emphasize.
- Choose a photo likely to stimulate discussion on the topic, and make it the focal point of a large poster prominently displayed in the classroom.
- Introduce the topic and ask students to talk briefly about some things they know about the topic. Have each student generate a list of words related to the topic and collect the lists. Then put the words the students generated on the poster.
- Take a virtual field trip with your class using the poster as your destination: Ask students for words describing what they see, hear, and feel. Add these words to the poster with Post-its, and group related words.
- Read the easiest book aloud. Have students give thumbs-up when they hear one of the words. (This seemingly tangential activity is an important part of the procedure, since it keeps students involved and focused on the key words.) Add key words to the poster if students don't supply them.
- Read the remaining books aloud in order of increasing difficulty, again having students give thumbs-up when they hear one of the words, and again adding key words

if students don't supply them. Reorganize the words as seems appropriate.

- Do extension activities such as word games, sorting, writing, and reading new topically related books.
- Evaluate students' learning by having them again generate a list of words related to the topic and comparing their initial lists with their final ones. As a less direct form of evaluation, you can also have students summarize their favorite of the books you read aloud or create their own books on the topic.

Figure 5.13 shows some of the core words Blachowicz and Obrochta identified for first graders working with the topic of *skeletons* (part of a unit on the human body), as well as some of the words students generated, while Figure 5.14 shows the books Blachowicz and Obrochta used while working with another group of first graders on the topic *recycling*.

ROBUST INSTRUCTION

Robust Instruction is a powerful procedure that has been developed and investigated by Beck and McKeown and their colleagues over some time (e.g., Beck & McKeown, 2007; Beck, Perfetti, & McKeown, 1982) and that is described in detail in Beck, McKeown, and Kucan (2002, 2008). Robust Instruction is designed to give students deep and lasting understanding of word meanings and is particularly appropriate and effective when used with interesting and somewhat intriguing words such as *banter, retort, glum, berate,* and *impatient*. Here is a version that can be used in a number of situations. For the sake of simplicity, this example deals with a single word—*ambitious*. Often, however, Robust Instruction is used to teach a set of words over a period of a week or so.

- Begin with a student-friendly definition.
  ambitious—really wanting to succeed at something
- Arrange for students to work with the word several times. One encounter with a word is very unlikely to leave students with a rich and lasting understanding of its meaning.
- Provide the word in more than one context so that students' understanding is not limited to one situation.

FIGURE 5.13. Some Core Words (in roman) and Student Supplied Words (in italics) for a Vocabulary Visits Session on *Skeletons*

bone	skull	leg	arm	wrist
ankle	foot	ribs	brain	spine
backbone	protect	*system*	*hollow*	*inside*
support	*elbow*	*skin*	*head*	*crown*
cranium	*joints*	*heart*	*lungs*	*shoulder*

FIGURE 5.14. Books Used with Vocabulary Visits on the Topic *Recycling*

Marx, D. (2001). *Earth Day* (Rookie Read-About Holidays). Chicago: Children's Press.

Gibbons, G. (1996). *Recycle: A Handbook for Kids*. New York: Little, Brown.

Robinson, F. (1996). *Too Much Trash* (Rookie Read-Aloud Science). Chicago: Children's Press.

Showers, P. (1994). *Where Does the Garbage Go?* New York: HarperCollins.

The several contexts need not come at the same time.

Susan's *ambition* to become an Olympic high jumper was so strong that she was willing to practice 6 hours a day.

Rupert had never been an *ambitious* person, and after his accident he did little other than watch television.

- Engage students in activities in which they need to deal with various facets of the word's meaning and in investigating relationships between the target word and other words.

Would you like to have a really *ambitious* person as a friend? Why or why not?

Which of the following better demonstrates *ambition*? (1) A stockbroker gets up every day and goes to work. (2) A stockbroker stays late at work every day, trying to close as many deals as possible before leaving.

How likely is it that an *ambitious* person would be *lethargic*? How likely is it that an *ambitious* person would be *energetic*? Explain your answers.

- Have students create uses for the words.

Tell me about a friend that you see as very *ambitious*. What are some of the things she does that show how *ambitious* she is?

- Encourage students to use the word outside of class. Come to class tomorrow prepared to talk about someone who appears to be ambitious. This could be a stranger you happen to notice outside of class, someone in your family, someone you read about, or someone you see on TV.

Quite obviously, Robust Instruction will create deep and lasting understanding of words. Equally obviously, Robust Instruction takes a great deal of time, certainly more time than you can spend on most words you teach. You will need to decide just which words merit its use.

KNOWLEDGE AS DESIGN

Knowledge as Design (Perkins, 1986, 1994) is a discussion procedure that serves to focus students' attention as they consider a topic. It is particularly useful when at least some students in the class already have some knowledge on a topic. As Perkins explains, four powerful questions can be used to explore and reveal the nature of any topic and therefore any word:

- What is the purpose of _____ ?
- What is the structure (or components of) _____ ?
- What are some examples of _____ ?
- What are some arguments for and against _____ ?

Despite its potential for investigating virtually any topic, the procedure is very straightforward and easily implemented:

- Explain to students that you are going to be using a discussion procedure called Knowledge as Design to explore concepts they are studying.
- Explain further that the procedure uses four questions to focus the discussion, and display the four design questions.
- Choose a concept to discuss. *Advertising* is one you might discuss with middle school students.
- Motivate students to investigate the topic under discussion. With advertising, you might focus on its huge presence in their lives.
- Put the topic and the four questions on the board, leaving

space for responses below each question. (Although you can conduct a Knowledge as Design Conversation using an overhead or LCD, I have found that a chalkboard works best.)

- Hold a class discussion on each of the four questions. Record responses on the board, and have students record them in a Design Conversation Worksheet like that shown in Figure 5.15, which shows a completed Design Conversation on *advertising*. The questions can come in whatever order seems to best fit the concept under discussion, but once you start on a question, finish it before going to another one. Initially, you may have to scaffold students' efforts by assuming much of the work of the discussion, but students will increasingly become independent.

- Once the four questions have been answered and the results recorded, give students an opportunity to synthesize the information they have produced, connect it to their existing knowledge, and draw conclusions. Figure 5.15 shows a possible conclusion for *advertising*.

Clearly, Knowledge as Design is another vocabulary procedure in which discussion takes center stage. In fact, Knowledge as Design is solely discussion, but it is a particularly powerful form of discussion because it is focused. I have used the procedure with excellent results with students from the elementary grades through college.

FRAYER METHOD

The Frayer Method (Frayer, Frederick, & Klausmeier, 1969) is a very powerful approach to teaching concepts; it is in fact the standard approach to teaching concepts. The procedure has six steps. Here, I list those steps and provide examples with the words/concepts *globe* and *perseverance*.

1. Define the new concept, giving its necessary attributes. When feasible, it is also helpful to show a picture illustrating the concept.
   - A *globe* is a spherical (ball-like) representation of a planet.

FIGURE 5.15. Completed Design Conversation Worksheet on *Advertising*

Purposes	Specific Examples
to get you to buy something to get you really interested in something to convince you that you need something to make money	TV ads for drugs, clothes, etc. billboard ads for soft drinks ads on the Internet and in magazines ads on clothes you wear
Structure	**Pro Arguments**
Sometimes they tell little stories. Sometimes they show someone really cool using the product. Sometimes a sports star or other star tells you about it. Sometimes they are funny.	They let you know about new products. Some are entertaining. They give you time to get up and get a snack. They keep you in the know.
Con Arguments	**Conclusion**
You buy things you don't want or need. You spend more money. It makes magazines really thick. Watching a movie takes forever. You see advertising everyplace you go.	There will probably always be advertising because people will want to sell things and there are some advantages to having advertising, but there are a lot of disadvantages and there is too much advertising.

- *Perseverance* is a trait that a person might possess. A person demonstrates *perseverance* when he or she remains constant to some purpose or task over some extended period despite obstacles.

2. Distinguish between the new concept and similar but different concepts for which it might be mistaken. In doing so, it may be appropriate to identify some accidental attributes that might falsely be considered to be necessary attributes of the new concept.

- A *globe* is different from a *map* because a map is flat. A *globe* is different from a *contour map*, a map in which mountains and other high points are raised above the general level of the map, because a contour map is not spherical.

• *Perseverance* differs from *stubbornness* in that *perseverance* is typically seen as a positive quality and the goal toward which one perseveres is typically a worthwhile one. Conversely, *stubbornness* is usually seen as a negative quality, and the goal pursued by a person who is being stubborn is often not a worthwhile one.

3. Give examples of the concept and explain why they are examples.

• The most common *globe* is a globe of the earth. Globes of the earth are spherical and come in various sizes and colors.

• A much less common *globe* is a globe of another planet. A museum might have a spherical representation of Saturn.

• A person who graduates from college despite financial responsibilities that require him or her to work full time while in college would be demonstrating *perseverance* because the goal is worthwhile and it takes a long and steady effort to reach it.

• A person who learns to ski after losing a leg in an accident is demonstrating *perseverance* for similar reasons.

4. Give nonexamples of the concept.
   • *For globe*:
      A map of California
      A map of how to get to a friend's house
   • *For perseverance*:
      Someone who goes fishing a lot just because he or she enjoys it is not demonstrating perseverance because there is no particular purpose here and no obstacles.

      Someone who waters his or her lawn once a week is not demonstrating *perseverance* because there is no particular challenge in doing so.

5. Present students with examples and nonexamples and ask them to distinguish between the two.
   • *For globe*:
      An aerial photograph of New York (nonexample)
      A red sphere representing Mars (example)

A walking map of St. Louis (nonexample)

A ball-shaped model of the moon (example)

- *For perseverance*:

Reading an interesting book that you thoroughly enjoy (nonexample)

Completing a canoe trip from the headwaters of the Mississippi to New Orleans (example)

Eating a dozen doughnuts because you are really hungry (nonexample)

Completing a 3-mile cross country race even though you were out of breath and dead tired after less than a mile (example)

6. Have students present examples and nonexamples of the concept, have them explain why they are examples or nonexamples, and give them feedback on their examples and explanations.

The Frayer Method has a number of strengths: It begins with a clear definition. It considers the concept a number of times and from a number of perspectives. It recognizes that understanding what something is necessarily involves understanding what it is not. It involves students in active processing. And it is a terrific example of gradual release of responsibility (Pearson & Gallagher, 1983): It begins with the teacher doing all of the work and gradually gives the students increasing work.

EXPRESSIVE VOCABULARY INSTRUCTION

Most of the procedures I have discussed in this chapter are designed primarily to build students' reading vocabularies. It also makes sense to give some attention to building students' writing vocabularies. Expressive Vocabulary Instruction (Duin & Graves, 1987, 1988) is modeled on the Robust Instruction developed by Beck and McKeown, which I discussed earlier; but it is modified to focus on getting students to actively use new and interesting words in their writing. The approach can be used with intermediate-grade through middle school students and works well when taught as a weeklong unit.

- Assemble a set of 10 or so related words. Not all of them need to be semantically related, but they do need to lend themselves to writing on a particular topic.

A set of words Duin used in conjunction with students writing an essay about *space* included *feasible, accommodate, tether, criteria, module, retrieve, configuration,* and *quest*

- Have students work extensively with the words, spending about half an hour a day with them over several days of instruction and doing 5 to 10 activities with each word.

  Some activities that would maintain students interest and give students opportunities to consider the words from different perspectives include

  defining the words
  using them in sentences
  discussing them
  doing speeded trials with them
  making affective responses to them
  comparing them to each other and to other concepts
  keeping a written record of work with them,
  using them outside of class
  doing several short writing assignments with them.

- Vary the activities to give students multiple opportunities to consider the words and to have students consider them from various perspectives. Among the varied activities Duin and Graves used in discussing space words were these: Students discussed how *feasible* space travel might soon be for each of them. They were asked if they thought their school could find a way to better *accommodate* handicapped students. They distinguished between new words, such as *retrieve*, and related words, such as *return*, by filling in sentence frames with the more appropriate of the two words. And they wrote brief essays called "Space Shorts," employing the words in dealing with such topics as how people could survive in space and the foods that would be available in space.

Students who received Expressive Vocabulary Instruction with the group of words relevant to space later wrote essays that included a substantial proportion of the taught words. Moreover, these students' essays were judged as markedly superior to those of students who had not received this instruction. Equally important, students thoroughly enjoy learning and using words in this way. Figure 5.16 displays an essay written by one Expressive Instruction student.

FIGURE 5.16. A Student's Space Essay Following Expressive Instruction (with taught words underlined)

I think the space program would be much more <u>feasible</u> if we sent more than just astronauts and satellites into space. We need to send tourists and change the whole <u>configuration</u> of the space shuttle so that it can <u>accommodate</u> more people. While the tourists are in space, they could fly some of the manned-maneuvering units and <u>retrieve</u> stuff from space. They could maybe even see if our planets are habitable now. When the tourists would come back, they would have the capability of doing anything in space. They would truly be advocates of space. But in order to make these special missions happen, we will need to add more <u>modules</u> onto our space station, so that we can store more equipment, supplies, food, and people.

After about ten years or so, we would perhaps go back to the same old thing with the astronauts and satellites until we found another new idea for the space program.

My <u>quest</u>, someday, is to reach the stars. I hope to be not just an engineer, but a space engineer. We have to get more people interested since the crash. We have to try harder than ever.

SUMMING UP

Although each of the 12 procedures described in this chapter has unique features and purposes and some of them take more time and produce deeper learning than others, all of them provide rich and powerful instruction that will leave students with deep and lasting word knowledge. In doing so, all of them give students a definition of the word, use the word in context, have students actively manipulate word meanings, involve discussion, and have students work with the word more than once. All of them represent exemplary instruction. Still, that does not mean that you need to use all of these techniques. Use those that best fit you and your students, that do the jobs you need done, and that provide the right balance of novelty and familiarity. Neither does the fact that these are exemplary mean that they are the only techniques to use. With 50,000 words to teach, you don't always have time for really rich instruction. Still, if you have a difficult concept that students need to learn well, teaching it is going to take some time. Teaching a new and difficult concept as though it is merely a new label—for example, teaching it using the Context-Dictionary-Discussion procedure described in Chapter 6—will not get the job done.

Introductory Instruction

The instructional procedures described in Chapter 5 are, as I have emphasized, very powerful procedures and ones that will leave students with deep and lasting word knowledge. However, as I have also noted, they are time consuming. With something like 50,000 words students need to learn, we cannot always spend a lot of time on each of the individual words that we teach. Moreover, often we do not need to. Frequently, it is appropriate and sufficient to give students introductory instruction, instruction that will start them on the long road to learning rich and deep meanings. In this chapter, I describe seven types of introductory instruction.

TEACHING STUDENTS TO READ KNOWN WORDS

The simplest vocabulary-teaching task is that of teaching students to read words that are already in their oral vocabularies. In this case, the student already knows the word and its meaning, he can understand it when he hears it and can probably (although not necessarily) use it in speaking. But he can't read it. The basic task for the student is to associate what is unknown, the written word, with what is already known, the spoken word. This is a basically a decoding task. Students need to associate the written word, which they do not recognize, with the spoken word, which they already know. To establish the association between the written and spoken forms of a word, students need to see the word at the same time that it is pronounced. Once this association is established, students need to rehearse it repeatedly so that the relationship becomes automatic. I have listed these steps below to emphasize just how straightforward the process is:

- See the word.
- Hear the word as it is seen.
- Rehearse that association myriad times.

Of course, there are many ways in which each of these steps can be accomplished. Students can see the word on the board, on a computer screen, or in a book that they are reading or you are reading to them. They can hear the word when you say it, when another student says it, or when a voice simulator on a computer says it. They can rehearse the association by seeing the word and pronouncing it a number of times, writing it, and playing games that require them to recognize printed versions of it. However, there is one best way to rehearse the association: Wide reading in materials that contain many repetitions of these words and that are enjoyable and easily read by students is by far the best form of rehearsal for these words and an essential part of students' mastering them. Of course, wide reading also serves myriad other purposes.

PROVIDING GLOSSARIES

Providing Glossaries is one of the least time consuming and least interruptive vocabulary-teaching techniques available. It entails just three steps:

- Identify key words in a selection students will be reading that they may not know.
- Write a student-friendly definition for each word.
- Give students the glossary, explain how to use it, and model using it yourself.

Glossaries can be created for both fiction and nonfiction selections, although they are particularly useful with nonfiction because they can focus on key content words. For example, a glossary for an intermediate-grade science chapter on weathering and erosion might include the words *delta, sediment, erosion, glacier, levee,* and *weathering*. A glossary for an intermediate-grade narrative, on the other hand, is likely to include a less closely related set of words, words like *temporarily, donate, maximum, ascend, disarray,* and *maintain*. Many glossaries you create are likely to be for short selections like chapters and short stories, but you can also create glossaries for longer works like chapter books and novels.

One of the advantages of glossaries is that they can include quite a few words, more than you would probably include with a more direct teaching technique. However, when you are working with relatively short selections, I would suggest some limits. For primary-grade students, I would suggest glossaries no larger than 5–10 words, for intermediate-grade students glossaries no larger than 10–15 words, and for middle-grade students glossaries no larger than 15–20 words.

When listing each word in the glossary, I typically divide it into syllables and show where the accent is but do not write it out phonetically. For each word, write a student-friendly definition following the suggestions in Chapter 3. Here are two examples of glossary definitions:

> *scur'-ry.* Scurry means to move at a fast pace, often rather nervously.
> *tsu-na'-mi.* A tsunami is a large wave that can occur after an underwater earthquake.

Although glossaries can be put on the chalkboard, I typically put them on handouts. Many students will have had some experience with glossaries. Nevertheless, the first time you use one in your class, it's a good idea to briefly describe glossaries and how to use them.

CONTEXT-DICTIONARY-DISCUSSION

Teaching Students to Read Known Words is, of course, only appropriate for words that are already in students' oral vocabularies, and Providing Glossaries is a passive form of instruction. This makes the Context-Dictionary-Discussion procedure the first full-fledged instructional procedure I discuss in this chapter. It is a brief and straightforward procedure and does not take much preparation on your part. It goes like this:

- Give students the word in context (the context it appears in in the material students are reading).
- Ask them to look it up in an age-appropriate dictionary.
- Discuss the definitions students come up with, and make certain they have an appropriate definition that they understand.

The examples below show sentence contexts for two words:

> To get into the Olympics, a person must really *excel at* some Olympic sport.
> Nicole, a student in Ms. Green's third-hour mathematics class, had used the term x to refer to three different quantities, and thus she added *subscripts* to tell the three terms apart.

The key to the success of this method is the discussion, one in which you want to make sure that students have an appropriate definition and one that they understand. Frequently, students will just take the first definition of the word they find in the dictionary, whether or not that definition fits the context in which the word occurred. Often, too, students will just consider part of a definition, usually the first few words. The discussion needs to be lengthy enough and engage enough students that you are confident students have a correct and reasonably complete understanding of the word. This means that although the procedure does not require much preparation on your part, it does require a fair amount of class time.

DEFINITION PLUS RICH CONTEXT

The Definition Plus Rich Context procedure provides about the same level of instruction as the Context-Dictionary-Discussion procedure, but it takes more out-of-class preparation time on your part and then less class time. It, too, is simple and straightforward.

- Create a student-friendly definition and a rich context for the word.
- Give students the definition and the context on the chalkboard, overhead, or LCD, and have them briefly consider them.
- Discuss the definition, the context, and some other contexts in which the word might be used.

Here are two examples of Definition Plus Rich Context items:

If something is *vital*, it is extremely important, perhaps even necessary.
In areas where water is very scarce, it is *vital* that everyone take extra precautions to ensure that no water is wasted.
Irradiate means to treat something or someone with radiation.
It's becoming increasingly common to *irradiate* meat and some other foods to kill potentially harmful bacteria.

DEFINITION, RICH CONTEXT, AND A PICTURE

This is just like the Definition Plus Rich Context procedure except that you add a picture along with the definition and the context. Of course, only some words can be pictured; but for those that can, pictures can be enormously helpful. Moreover, pictures can be particularly beneficial for English learners. Consider, for example, the definition and context for the word *avalanche* in Figure 6.1.

This is an informative definition and a rich context, and together they will provide students with a basic meaning of *avalanche*. But it is not a particularly full meaning. Now consider the same definition and rich context along with the picture of an avalanche shown in the figure. I think you will agree that students will have a much fuller understanding of *avalanche* with the picture than without it. Moreover, with the availability of pictures on the Internet, you have easy access to a huge collection of pictures. Google Image, for example, lists well over a million images of avalanches. Making use of an image can markedly improve students' understanding of a word, make the instruction more interesting, and better cement the word in students' memories. Additionally, if you have an LCD pro-

FIGURE 6.1. Definition, Rich Context, and a Picture Item for the Word
  Avalanche **(Photo courtesy of the National Park Service)**

An *avalanche* occurs when a large mass of snow and rock slide very rapidly down a mountain. It can be very destructive.

When the skiers saw the *avalanche* coming, they were terrified and headed for cover just as fast as they could go.

jector in your classroom, and increasing numbers of classrooms do, showing images from the Internet becomes really easy. Figure 6.2 shows another Definition, Rich Context, and a Picture item, this one for the word *scaffold*.

CONTEXT-RELATIONSHIP

The Context-Relationship procedure (Graves & Slater, 2008), takes more preparation time on your part than the other methods discussed in this chapter. Once you have selected a word, you have to create a well-crafted paragraph that uses the word several times. However, presenting a word in this way takes only about a minute of class time, making it very efficient from that perspective. Here is how it is done:

- Create a brief paragraph that uses the target word three or four times and in doing so gives the meaning of the word.
- Follow the paragraph with a three-option, multiple-choice item that checks students' understanding of the word.
- Show the paragraph (probably on an overhead or LCD),

FIGURE 6.2. Definition, Rich Context, and a Picture Item for the Word *Scaffold*

A *scaffold* is a temporary structure that holds something up while it is being built.

There was so much *scaffolding* around the building as it was being built that it was difficult to tell what the building really looked like.

read it aloud, and read the multiple-choice options.

- Pause to give students a moment to answer the multiple-choice item, give them the correct answer, and discuss the word and any questions they have.

Figure 6.3 contains examples with the words *conveying* and *rationale*. I have written a number of these items and have learned a few things to keep in mind. First, while the first two or three sentences of the paragraph simply use the word, the last sentence generally defines it. Second, although these examples use only one form of the words—*conveying* on the one hand and *rationale* on the other—it works equally wall to use various forms. For *conveying*, for example, you could use *convey, conveyed,* and *conveys.* Third, the distractors in the multiple-choice items should be the same part of speech as each other. Also, while they should not be silly and clearly inappropriate, they should be distinctly wrong. This is not a procedure for teaching fine gradations of meaning.

TEACHING NEW MEANINGS FOR KNOWN WORDS

Teaching New Meanings for Known Words, the last procedure I describe in this chapter, is designed for situations in which stu-

FIGURE 6.3. Context-Relationship Items for the Words *Conveying* and *Rationale*

Conveying

The luncheon speaker was successful in *conveying* his main ideas to the audience. They all understood what he said, and most agreed with him. *Conveying* has a more specific meaning than *talking*. *Conveying* indicates that a person is getting his or her ideas across accurately.
Conveying means
____ A. putting parts together
____ B. communicating a message
____ C. hiding important information

Rationale

The *rationale* for my wanting to expose students to a variety of words and their meanings is partially that this will help them become better thinkers who are able to express their ideas more clearly. Part of that *rationale* also includes my belief that words themselves are fascinating objects of study. My *rationale* for doing something means my fundamental reasons for doing it.
Rationale means
_____ A. a deliberate error
_____ B. the basis for doing something
_____ C. a main idea for an essay

---

dents already know one meaning of a word and you want to teach a meaning that they do not know.

- Acknowledge the known meaning. Give a brief student-friendly definition of it and use it in a sentence.
- Give the new meaning, again using a student-friendly definition and a sentence context.
- Discuss the similarities between the two meanings or specifically note that there are no similarities.

Figure 6.4 presents an example with the word *product*, and Figure 6.5 an example with the word *main*. Note that with the word *product* the new meaning is specific to math, while with the word *main* the new meaning is not a content-specific word. Note also that contrasting the new meaning with the known one is a very important part of the technique, so be sure to include this step.

FIGURE 6.4. Dialogue for Teaching a New Meaning for the Word *Product*

You all know the word *product* meaning "something people make so that they can sell it." This is the meaning *product* has in the sentence, "Many people think that Sony makes a pretty good *product*."

The word *product* also has another meaning, a special meaning used in math. In math the word *product* refers to "the number you get when you multiply other numbers." This is the meaning of *product* in the sentence, "The *product* of 3 x 4 is 12."

The similarity of the two meanings is that in both cases *product* refers to something that is made. The more general word *product* refers to something that is made by a person or a company, while the word *product* in math refers to the number that is made by multiplying other numbers.

FIGURE 6.5. Dialogue for Teaching a New Meaning for the Word Main

---

You all know the word *main* meaning "more important." This is the meaning *main* has in the sentence, "The main character in the book is a troubled teenager."

The word *main* also has another meaning. It can mean "the open sea." This is the meaning of *main* in the sentence, "In the 17th century, pirates sailed the *main* in search of ships to capture and plunder." This latter meaning is seldom used in regular speech today, although it is sometimes used in literature.

The similarity of the two meanings is that in both cases *main* refers to something that is important. In one case, it refers to anything important, and in the other case it refers to the open sea, which is more important or at least larger than smaller bodies of water, such as bays or inlets.

SUMMING UP

This has been a brief chapter because each of the seven techniques I suggest for teaching individual words is relatively brief. That does not mean, however, that they all serve the same purpose. Teaching Students to Read Known Words is designed for teaching words already in students' oral vocabularies; Providing Glossaries gives students the opportunity to work independently; and Teaching New Meanings for Known Words, of course, teaches new meanings for words students already know one meaning for. The other techniques serve basically the same purpose but differ in other ways.

The Context-Dictionary-Discussion method requires very little preparation on your part but quite a bit of class time; the Definition Plus Rich Context procedure requires somewhat more preparation; the Definition, Rich Context, and a Picture procedure adds a visual element; and the Context-Relationship procedure takes quite a bit of preparation but not much class time. You will need to pick among these techniques to choose those that do the job you need done, require the mix of out-of-class preparation and in-class time you find appropriate, and are good matches for you and your students. Of course, you may also want to use several different techniques just to provide variety. Whichever ones you choose to use, you are likely to use introductory techniques often because there are a lot of words to which students need introductions.

Repetition, Assessment, and Differences Across Grade Levels

The previous six chapters have presented much of what I have to say about teaching individual words. In Chapter 1, I discussed the importance of vocabularies, the limited vocabularies of linguistically less advantaged children, and a comprehensive four-part program, of which teaching individual words is just one part. In Chapter 2, I discussed information important to understand as you plan instruction on individual words. In Chapter 3, I discussed considerations to take into account for all types of instruction on individual words, considerations such as selecting vocabulary to teach and the vocabulary-learning task of English learners. Chapter 4 described ways of building students' oral vocabulary, something crucial to students who enter school with very small vocabularies. Chapter 5 described rich and powerful instruction on reading vocabulary, while Chapter 6 described introductory instruction on reading vocabulary. I conclude this book by discussing three topics: the importance of repetition, assessing word knowledge, and differences in vocabulary instruction across the grades. Following that, I make a few final comments about teaching individual words and about vocabulary instruction more generally.

THE IMPORTANCE OF REPETITION

Learning words is a gradual thing. The first encounter a student has with a word leaves her with some part of the word's meaning, and each additional encounter rewards her with a richer and more precise meaning. Each of the procedures for building students' oral vocabularies presented in Chapter 4 and each of the procedures for rich and powerful instruction presented in Chapter 5 provide students with multiple encounters with the words being taught, while the procedures for introductory instruction presented in Chapter 6 provide students with a single or perhaps a few encounters. Ensuring that students remember the words they are taught with introductory techniques definitely requires that we plan additional encounters with the words, and even those words taught with rich and powerful instruction that provides multiple encounters are more likely to remain in students' vocabularies if students encounter them again over time. Some additional encounters are likely to come as students are reading and in discussion, but there is no guarantee how often this will happen. Of course, you cannot provide repetition for all the words you teach. Time does not allow it. A major theme of this book is that there are so many words to learn that some of them need to be dealt with briefly. But when time does allow it, repetition is a very good thing.

Sometimes, the repetition can be very brief and simply embedded in class discussion. For example, noting that the word *catastrophic*, which you have previously taught, appears again in the selection students are reading, you might say something like, "You might have noticed that the word *catastrophic*, which we learned several weeks ago, comes up again in today's chapter. Again, a *cata-*

strophic event is a really serious event, something that would produce widespread damage, like a hurricane."

At other times, repetition will involve specific procedures.
Richek (2005) has described three time-efficient procedures for reviewing words students have already been taught, and Beck, Perfetti, and McKeown (1982) have described one. Here, I describe
slightly modified forms of each of these.

Anything Goes

With Anything Goes, you begin by prominently displaying the
words to be reviewed where everyone in the class can see them and
explaining to students that occasionally you are going to point to
some of the words displayed and ask questions about them. Often
you'll post a particular set of words for a week, but you can certainly put them up for a longer or shorter period. Once the words
are posted, you can ask students to do any of the following:

- Define the word
- Give two of its meanings
- Use it in a sentence
- Give an example of the thing named or described by the
  word
- Say where you would find the word or the thing named or
  described by the word
- Explain the difference between two of the words, or
  between one of the words on the list and some other word
- Give the past tense, plural, or *-ing* form of a base word
- Give the root for words with prefixes or suffixes
- Give prefixed or suffixed forms of root words

Note that you certainly don't use all of these with any one word.
You'll typically use two or three of them with each word—whatever seems enough. Suppose the list for third graders included 10
words, among which were *melody, agenda,* and *mention.* You might
ask students to define *melody,* give an example of a melody, and
say where they might hear a melody. Then you might ask them
to use *agenda* in a sentence, tell you where they are likely to find
an agenda, and say the plural of *agenda.* After that, you might ask
them to use the word *mention* in a sentence, tell you something that
they might mention to a friend, and explain the difference between

"mentioning" something and "discussing" something. Typically, I've found it convenient to review three to six words in this way at one time, but you can certainly do more or fewer when that seems appropriate.

Once you have worked with Anything Goes enough that you think most of your students understand the way it works, you may want to post the list of prompts on the board, discuss them, and invite students to sometimes do the prompting. If you do this, you can save class time by sending the list home with students and asking them to prepare prompts for two or three of the words. Of course, you can always make generating prompts group work. The time the groups spend generating prompts is likely to be well spent, although this will increase the time spent on the review significantly.

Connect Two

With Connect Two, you give students two columns of perhaps 10 words each and ask students to identify similarities or other relationships between a word in column 1 and a word in column 2. Here are some words that Richek (2005) used with fifth graders.

Column 1	Column 2
bayonet	hoarse
disgrace	exuberant
muffled	cunning
exposed	pondered
insignificant	ruefully
splendid	courier
roll	musket
magazine	incense
ravine	restrain

As Richek points out, children may at first come up with relationships that are superficial, such as that *bayonet* and *cunning* have the same number of letters. That is fine to start with, but what you want to encourage is children searching for meaningful relationships that require deep processing. Modeling can be useful here, as it so frequently is, so you may want to explain that you are looking for deeper relationships and model a few of those. You might, for example, note that *muffled* and *hoarse* have to do with sound, that a person is not likely to be *exuberant* about being *disgraced*, and that a *bayonet* might be attached to a *musket*. Soon, children will begin finding meaningful relationships, and the thought processes they engage in while doing so will help them remember the words and deepen their understanding of them.

Two in One

Two in One is similar to Connect Two, but in this case you have students write sentences that use two of the words you're reviewing. While the common activity of writing a sentence using a single vocabulary word does not require much thought, it turns out that writing a sentence with two vocabulary words in it often requires quite a bit of thought. This mental effort makes Two in One a powerful review activity. Consider, for example, the words *prestigious* and *enunciate*. Now close the book, think a minute, and write out a sentence that uses both of them. I suspect that coming up with a sentence took you a little thought, forcing you to ponder the meaning of the two words as you tried to come up with a sentence that included both of them. It certainly took me a little thought. Here is the sentence I came up with, "I was surprised when a *prestigious* senator failed to *enunciate* properly." It's not a great sentence, and I would not be surprised if you came up with a better one. But regardless of the beauty of the sentences we came up with, we had to think hard on the meanings of the two words to create them, and that is the point. Here are a few sentences some eighth graders came up with for the words *collage* and *gullible*, *induct* and *mulligan*, and *redeem* and *sulk*.

- I'd say that you would have to be pretty *gullible* to pay a lot for a *collage*.
- My mother *inducted* my new boyfriend into our Irish family by serving him *mulligan* stew.
- After several days of *sulking* around the house, Will tried to *redeem* himself by being extra-pleasant.

You'll note that two of these sentences used inflected forms of the words. Allowing inflected forms is helpful in trying to create sentences. Something else that is often helpful is having students work in pairs or small groups. Still another thing that some students might want to try is using more than two vocabulary words in a sentence. Although using two vocabulary words in the same sentence will prove challenging for many students, others may decide they need an even more challenging task. This, of course, is great—and something to encourage.

Word Wizard

Word Wizard is an activity developed by Beck and her colleagues some years ago (Beck et al., 1982) and now widely used by teachers everywhere. It is almost too simple. You give students a list of the words they are reviewing and ask them to find the words used outside of class. When students find a word, they record the context in which it is used and report their finds in class, earning a point for each instance they report. In their work, which was with fourth graders, Beck and her colleagues went all out to make Word Wizard a big deal. They first advertised the notion by creating and distributing leaflets titled "You Can Be a Word Wizard." One part of the leaflet, which included engaging graphics, described what a Word Wizard was and the various levels of word wizardry students could achieve by earning points. These included Word Wildcat, Word Whirlwind, Word Winner, Word Worker, and Word Watcher, along with the ultimate level Word Wizard. Another part of the leaflet explained how points are earned:

> If you hear a word—on TV, on the radio, on the street, or at home [today of course we would add on a video, a CD, your iPod, or the Internet]—you can earn one point. Just tell your teacher where you heard or saw the word and how it was used. (Beck, McKeown, & Kucan, 2002, p. 119)

On the back of the leaflet, students were reminded to look for their name on the Word Wizard chart. The Word Wizard chart was a large and colorful chart with students' names and space for tallying their sightings of words. In class, students' sightings were heartily celebrated, and much was made of their efforts displayed on the chart. All in all, the activity was really well received by the students and engendered a lot of interest in vocabulary. In fact, Beck and her colleagues' comment that the children "went absolutely wild with bringing in the words." This has proven to be the case in other contexts. A colleague and I (Duin & Graves, 1987) used a similar but less elaborate version of Word Wizard with seventh graders and found that they loved it. Richek (2005) used a version with sixth graders and discovered that it "dramatically increases student awareness and appreciation for vocabulary words." Richek also reported success with the procedure when a primary-grade ELL teacher used it to reinforce common words like *bed*, *table*, and *television*.

ASSESSING WORD KNOWLEDGE

If you are going to spend your time and your students' time teaching individual words, you want to know which words they know and which words they don't. That way, you don't spend time "teaching" students words they already know or failing to teach words they don't know. Of course, with tens of thousands of words to learn, you can't check students' knowledge of each word before deciding whether to teach it. But you can get some idea of the size of each of your student's vocabularies relative to those of other students by using a standardized test. You can also get some idea of your students' knowledge of specific sets of words—for example, *The First 4,000 Words* (Graves, Sales, & Ruda, 2008), *Words Worth Teaching in Grades Three-Six* (Biemiller, in press), or the challenging words in a selection that students will be reading—with teacher-made tests. To be sure, the knowledge you gain from standardized tests or tests you create is not going to be in-depth knowledge. As Pearson, Hiebert, and Kamil (2007) recently explained, we are a long way from being able to create fine-grained vocabulary tests. But you can certainly get some idea of your students' word knowledge, and this can avoid a lot of wasted time and effort. Here, I describe five tests that can be useful. Two of them are commercial tests, and three of them are teacher made. One of them is individually administered, and the others are group tests.

Peabody Picture Vocabulary Test

The Peabody Picture Vocabulary Test IV (PPVT-4; Dunn & Dunn, 2007) is an individualized test of listening vocabulary. Although testing a single student takes only about 15 minutes, giving the test to a class is time consuming just because it is individualized. The PPVT-4 is something you would probably use only if you have some students you suspect of having very small vocabularies relative to their peers. The PPVT-4 can be used with a range of ages; so while you are probably most likely to use it with primary-grade children, you could also use it with older students. Like all the tests described here, the PPVT-4 needs to be interpreted with caution when used with English learners. The test is a series of sets of four pictures representing words of increasing difficulty. In giving the test, you sit with a child, say a word, and ask him to point to the picture represented by the word. Norms for the latest version of the test were developed in 2006–2007 and appear to appropriately represent today's U. S. population. Scores available include standard scores for age and grade, growth scale values, percentiles, stanines, normal curve equivalents, and age and grade equivalents. An item similar to those used in the PPVT is shown in Figure 7.1. The word being tested is *grapes*.

Two-Sentence Procedure

In order to provide a less time consuming way of measuring listening vocabulary in young children, Kearns and Biemiller (2007) have recently developed a group administered procedure that they have validated with K–2 children. This is not a test but a procedure that you can use in creating your own test. It is simple, straightforward, and produces scores quite similar to those produced with the more time consuming PPVT-4. Here is how it works.

- Identify a set of words you want to test. This will typically consist of 10–20 words.
- Write two sentences for each word, one of which is a true statement about the word and the other of which is a false statement about it.
- Arrange the sentences in a list in such a way that the two sentences on the same word are separated by several other sentences.
- Put a picture of an object such a face, bicycle, or hand next to each sentence so that you can tell students who cannot yet read numbers which sentence you are reading. Two "yes" sentences and two "no" sentences for the words *feather* and *vegetable* are shown in Figure 7.2.
- Give students a sheet with the sentence identifiers, the

FIGURE 7.1. Sample Item Similar to Those Used in the PPVT

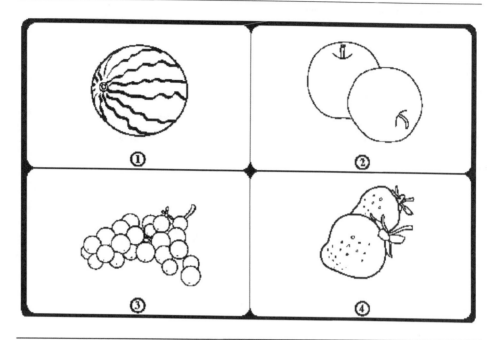

sentence numbers, and smiley (yes) faces and frowning (no) faces. The items the student sees for the four sample sentences are also shown in Figure 7.2.

- Explain the test to students. Say the name of each identifier and the item number to orient students, read the accompanying word and sentence to students, and give students time to fill in the "yes" face or the "no" face. For example, you might say, "Look at the face line, line 2. The word is *feather*. Is a feather part of a fish? Fill in the smiley face for "yes" or the frowning face for "no."

In a recent conversation I had with Beimiller, he noted that K–2 children are quite capable of taking the test, so, of course, older students would be, too. He tested kindergartners on 44 items (22 words) on two consecutive days. Giving the directions and the 22 items on the first day took about 45 minutes, but then giving the remaining 22 items the next day took only about 20 minutes. This, of course, is markedly less time than giving an individualized test to a class of 20–30 students would take. Remember that although the "yes" and "no" sentences for the word in Figure 7.2 appear close

FIGURE 7.2. Sample Item Illustrating Kearns and Biemiller's (2007) Two-Sentence Procedure

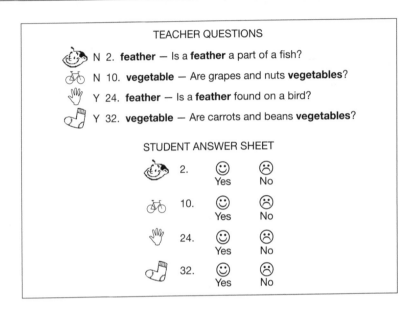

together in this sample, they need to be separated by quite a few items in an actual test.

Gates-MacGinitie Vocabulary Tests

The Gates-MacGinitie Reading Tests (MacGinitie, MacGinitie, Maria, Dreyer, & Hughes, 2000) are group-administered, norm-referenced reading tests that comes in a variety of levels from pre-reading through adult. The earliest levels do not include a test of reading vocabulary, but the tests for grade 2 and higher do, and the vocabulary test can be given by itself. Norms for the latest version of the test were developed in 2006 and appear to appropriately represent today's U. S. population. Scores available include normal curve equivalent, percentile rank, stanine, grade equivalent, and extended scale score, and these are available for the vocabulary subtest as well as for the other subtests and the total score. An item similar to those used in the Gates-MacGinitie is shown in Figure 7.3. The test is easy to administer to a classroom-size group and includes complete directions. Giving the vocabulary test takes about 20 minutes, and the results will give you an idea about your students' general vocabulary development relevant to other students in the class and their peers around the country.

FIGURE 7.3. Sample Item Similar to Those Used in the Gates-MacGinitie

It was an interesting *era.*
- kind of food
- type of sport
- period of time
- way of talking

Multiple-Choice Items

Another option for testing reading vocabulary is to construct and administer your own test. Typically, you construct such a test from a specific group of words—for example, *The First 4,000 Words* (Graves et al., 2008), the potentially difficult words in an upcoming reading selection, or the glossary of a textbook you are using. This makes it possible to draw conclusions such as "Almost all of my students can read all of the first 4,000 most frequent words," "Kimberly cannot read any of the words I identified as potentially difficult in Will Hobbs's *Crossing the Wire*," or "It looks like my class knows about half of the words that are glossed in our health text." In constructing such a test, I suggest making three-option multiple-choice items following these guidelines.

- Keep things simple and uncomplicated for yourself and your students. For example, make the question stem simply the word you are testing.
- Make the correct answer a clear and concise definition, doing everything you can to keep the words in the answer simpler than the word you are testing.
- Make the two distractors distinctly wrong. This is not the place for testing fine distinctions in meaning.
- While the distractors should be distinctly wrong, they should not be obviously wrong. All three alternatives should be about the same length and use the same syntax. Avoid alternatives that are silly or otherwise blatantly incorrect.

A sample item you might use with third graders and an item you might use with sixth graders are shown in Figure 7.4.

In addition to testing students on their word knowledge, you can use a multiple-choice test to check your knowledge of which words your students do and do not know. By constructing and giv-

FIGURE 7.4. Sample Multiple-Choice Items

Grade 3	Grade 6
1. dignified	2. fanatic
a. very hungry	a. very unreasonable
b. important looking	b. most acceptable
c. often late	c. sometimes unhealthy

ing a test with five words you are pretty sure most of your students know, five words you are pretty sure most of them don't know, and five you are uncertain about, you can readily find out how much you know about your students' vocabularies. If their performance squares with your predictions, great. If it does not, you need to work at learning more about their word knowledge. Only when you have a pretty good sense of the words your students are and are not likely to know can you effectively choose words to teach.

Student Self-Reporting

When time constraints make it impossible to create an actual test, there is a satisfactory alternative. Simply create, duplicate, and hand out a list of words. Give students the list, and explain what they are to do and the purpose of the exercise. What they are to do is put a checkmark beside the words they know. The purpose of their doing so—and it's really important to stress this—is for them to indicate whether they know each word so that you can teach those they don't know. It is not to give them a grade or in any way penalize them for not knowing some of them. In case you are suspicious of this approach, I should note that research by two colleagues and me (White, Slater, & Graves, 1989) showed that students are quite adept and truthful in identifying words they don't know in this way.

DIFFERENCES ACROSS GRADE LEVELS

There is a lot about teaching individual words that remains the same across the grade levels. For example, powerful instruction for first graders has the same characteristics as powerful instruction for eighth graders. However, there are a few things that are different across the grades, and recognizing these differences and adjusting instruction across the grades is important.

Primary Grades

In the primary grades, attention to oral vocabulary is particularly important. This means a lot of attention to the talk you use in the classroom and to the talk you encourage students to use. It also means that shared book reading is something to seriously consider for your students with very small vocabularies. In these same grades, you will frequently want to consider whether a word that may be merely a label to some students represents a new concept for others and needs to be taught accordingly. This is particularly true for some English learners. The primary grades are also the place where the most basic form of introductory instruction, Teaching Students to Read Known Words (see Chapter 6), is likely to be quite common.

Intermediate Grades

In the intermediate grades, oral vocabulary continues to be important, but reading vocabulary assumes increased emphasis. Shared book reading or other formal attempts to build oral vocabulary are therefore less likely. Similarly, because most students will have mastered or largely mastered decoding skills, Teaching Students to Read Known Words will not be needed with most words or most students. All other types of rich and powerful instruction and introductory instruction are likely to be useful. As students do increased work in content subjects like social studies and science, the content-specific vocabulary of these subjects becomes increasingly important and will require techniques like Four Squares and Possible Sentences (see Chapter 5).

Middle Grades

Word-learning strategies—such as using context, word parts, the dictionary, and (for Spanish speakers) idioms—are likely to have been taught before students enter the middle grades. If students have learned these strategies, then they can now use them at least some of the time, leaving you fewer words that need to be directly taught. This means you can and should give more attention to content-specific words; each year, as students deal with increasingly sophisticated material, there will be more of these. It also means that you can afford to give more attention to the challenging and time-consuming task of teaching concepts; for this, procedures like Knowledge as Design and the Frayer Method (see Chapter 5) should be particularly valuable.

FINAL COMMENTS

As the eminent psychologist George Miller (1956) pointed out more than 50 years ago in a classic article titled "The Magic Number Seven, Plus or Minus Two," human beings can readily remember about seven items. This seems a reasonable number of points to leave you with, so I will stick to that limit. (1) Vocabulary is tremendously important to success in and out of school. (2) Many students—linguistically advantaged ones—learn a tremendous number of words, accumulating vocabularies of something like 50,000 words by the time they graduate from high school. (3) Other students—linguistically less advantaged ones—learn many fewer words, and their smaller vocabularies are a very serious detriment to their success in school and in the world beyond school. (4) All students need help in learning the very large reading vocabulary they need to acquire, all students will profit from help in acquiring a large oral vocabulary, and some students need special help in building oral vocabulary as well as in building reading vocabulary. (5) With 50,000 words that need to be learned, we cannot spend a lot of time on each of these words, and fortunately we do not need to. (6) Some words can be taught with procedures specifically designed for teaching oral vocabulary, other words can be taught with rich and powerful instruction, and still others can be taught with introductory instruction. However words are initially taught, repetition will help fix them in students' memories. (7) Finally, there is the matter of testing. With the number of words that need to be taught, it is important to avoid "teaching" words students already know. To do so, judicious use of both commercial and teacher-made tests is crucial.

References and Children's Literature

American Heritage Dictionary. (4th ed.). (2001). Boston: Houghton Mifflin.

Anderson, R. C., Hiebert, E. H., Scott, J. A., & Wilkinson, I. A. G. (1985). *Becoming a nation of readers.* Washington, DC: National Academy of Education.

Anderson, R. C., & Nagy, W. E. (1992). The vocabulary conundrum. *American Educator,* Winter, 14–18, 44–47.

Anglin, J. M. (1993). Vocabulary development: A morphological analysis. *Monographs of the Society for Research in Child Development, 58* (Serial No. 238).

August, D., & Shanahan, T. (Eds.). (2006). *Developing literacy in second-language learners: Report of the National Literacy Panel on Language-Minority Children and Youth.* Mahwah, NJ: Lawrence Erlbaum.

August, D., & Snow, C. (2007). Developing vocabulary in English-language learners: A review of the experimental research. In B. M. Taylor & J. E. Ysseldyke (Eds.), *Effective instruction for struggling readers, K–6* (pp. 84–105). New York: Teachers College Press.

Avi. (1990). *True confessions of Charlotte Doyle.* New York: Orchard.

Avi. (2002). *Crispin: The cross of lead.* New York: Hyperion.

Babbit, N. (1975). *Tuck everlasting.* New York: Farrar, Straus and Giroux.

Base, G. (1986). *Anamalia.* New York: Harry N. Abrams.

Beck, I. L., & McKeown, M. G. (2001). Text talk: Capturing the benefits of read-aloud experiences for young children. *The Reading Teacher, 55,* 10–20.

Beck, I. L., & McKeown, M. G. (2007). Increasing young children's oral vocabulary repertoires through rich and focused instruction. *Elementary School Journal, 107,* 251–271.

Beck, I. L., McKeown, M. G., & Kucan, L. (2002). *Bringing words to life: Robust vocabulary instruction.* New York: Guilford.

Beck, I. L., McKeown, M. G., & Kucan, L. (2008). *Creating robust vocabulary: Frequently asked questions and extended examples.* New York: Guilford.

Beck, I. L., Perfetti, C. A., & McKeown, M. G. (1982). The effects of long-term vocabulary instruction on lexical access and reading comprehension. *Journal of Educational Psychology, 74,* 506–521.

Becker, W. C. (1977). Teaching reading and language to the disadvantaged—What we have learned from field research. *Harvard Educational Review, 47,* 511–543.

Biemiller, A. (2001, Spring). Teaching vocabulary: Early, direct, and sequential. *American Educator, 25* (1), 24–28, 47.

Biemiller, A. (2003, April). *Teaching vocabulary to kindergarten to grade two children.* Paper presented at the annual meeting of the American Educational Research Association, Chicago.

Biemiller, A. (2004). Teaching vocabulary in the primary grades: Vocabulary instruction needed. In J. F. Baumann & E. J. Kame'enui (Eds.), *Vocabulary instruction: Research to practice* (pp. 28–40). New York: Guilford.

Biemiller, A. (2005). Addressing developmental patterns in vocabulary: Implications for choosing words for primary grade vocabulary instruction. In E. H. Hiebert & M. L. Kamil (Eds.), *Teaching and learning vocabulary: Bringing research to practice: Vocabulary* (pp. 223–242). Mahwah, NJ: Erlbaum.

Biemiller, A. (in press). *Words worth teaching.* Columbus, OH: SRA/ McGraw-Hill.

Biemiller, A., & Boote, C. (2006). An effective method for building meaning vocabulary in primary grades. *Journal of Educational Psychology, 98,* 44–62.

Biemiller, A., & Slonim, N. (2001). Estimating root word and normative vocabulary growth in normative and advanced populations. Evidence for a common sequence of vocabulary acquisition. *Journal of Educational Psychology, 93,* 498–520.

Birdwell, N. (1977). *Clifford at the circus.* New York: Scholastic.

Blachowicz, C. L. Z., & Obrochta, C. (2005). Vocabulary visits: Virtual field trips for content vocabulary development. *The Reading Teacher, 59,* 262–268.

Blachowicz, C., & Obrochta, C. (2007). "Tweeking practice": Modifying read-alouds to enhance content vocabulary learning in grade 1. In J. Worthy, B. Maloch, J. V. Hoffman, D. L. Schallert, & C. M. Fairbanks. *56th Yearbook of the National Reading Conference* (pp. 111–121). Oak Creek, WI: National Reading Conference.

Calfee, R. C., & Drum, P. A. (1986). Research on teaching reading. In M.D. Wittrock (Ed.), *Handbook of research on teaching* (3rd ed.) (pp. 804–849). New York: Macmillan.

Carroll, J. B. (1971). *Learning from verbal discourse in educational media. A review of the literature.* Princeton, NJ: Educational Testing Service.

Carroll, J. B, Davies, P., & Richman, B. (1971). *The American Heritage word frequency book.* New York: Houghton Mifflin.

Chall, J. S., & Jacobs, V. A. (2003). The classic study on poor children's fourth-grade slump. *American Educator, 27*(1), 14–15, 44.

Chall, J. S., Jacobs, V. A., & Baldwin, L. E. (1990). *The reading crisis: Why poor children fall behind.* Cambridge, MA: Harvard University Press.

Clements, A. (1997). *Double trouble in Walla Walla.* Brookfield, CT: Millbrook.

Collins COBUILD new student's dictionary (3rd ed.). (2005). Glasgow, Scotland: HarperCollins.

Creech, S. (1994). *Walk two moons.* New York: HarperCollins.

Cronbach, L. J. (1942). An analysis of techniques for diagnostic vocabulary testing. *Journal of Educational Research, 36,* 206–217.

Cummins, J. (2003). Reading and the bilingual student: Fact and friction. In G. G. Garcia (Ed.), *English learners: Reaching the highest level of English literacy* (pp. 2–33). Newark, DE: International Reading Association.

Dale, E., & O'Rourke, J. (1981). *The living word vocabulary.* Chicago: World Book–Childcraft International.

De Temple, J., & Snow, C. E. (2003). Learning words from books. In A. van Kleeck, S. A. Stahl, and E. B. Bauer (Eds.), *On reading books to children* (pp. 16–36). Mahwah, NJ: Erlbaum.

Duin, A. H., & Graves, M. F. (1987). The effects of intensive vocabulary instruction on expository writing. *Reading Research Quarterly, 22,* 311–330.

Duin, A. H., & Graves, M. F. (1988). Teaching vocabulary as a writing prompt. *Journal of Reading, 22,* 204–212.

Dunn, L. M., & Dunn, D. M. (2007). *Peabody picture vocabulary test* (4th ed.). Minneapolis: Pearson Assessments.

Dupuy, H. (1974). *The rationale, development, and standardization of a basic word vocabulary test* (DHEW Publications N0. HRA74-1334). Washington, DC: U. S. Government Printing Office.

Faulkner, W. F. (1995). A rose for Emily. In E. McDonald (Ed.), *Collected stories of William Faulkner* (pp. 207–220). New York: Random House.

Fitzgerald, J. & Graves, M. F. (2004). *Scaffolding reading experiences for English language learners.* Norwood, MA: Christopher-Gordon.

Frayer, D. A., Frederick, W. D., & Klausmeier, H. J. (1969). *A schema for testing the level of concept mastery* (Working Paper No. 16). Madison: Wisconsin Research and Development Center for Cognitive Learning.

Freeman, D. (1978). *A pocket for Corduroy.* New York: Viking.

Gersten, R., & Baker, S. (2000). What we know about effective instructional practices for English-language learners. *Exceptional Children, 66,* 454–470.

Gibbons, G. (2003). *Grizzly bears.* New York: Holiday House.

Giblin, J. C. (1997). *Charles A. Lindbergh: A human hero.* New York: Clarion Books.

Gillman, P. (1997). *Jillian Jiggs.* New York: Scholastic.

Goldenberg, C. (2008). Teaching English learners: What the research does and does not say. *American Educator, 32*(1), 8–11, 14–19, 22–23, 42.

Goldenberg, C. (in press). Improving achievement for English Learners: Conclusions from recent reviews and emerging research. In S. Neuman (Ed.), *Literacy achievement for young children from poverty.* Baltimore, Brookes.

Goodall, J. (2001). *The chimpanzees I love: Saving their world and ours*. New York: Scholastic.

Graves, M. F. (1984). Selecting vocabulary to teach in the intermediate and secondary grades. In J. Flood (Ed.), *Understanding reading comprehension* (pp. 245–260). Newark, DE: International Reading Association.

Graves, M. F. (1985). *A word is a word . . . Or is it?* New York: Scholastic.

Graves, M. F. (1986). Vocabulary learning and instruction. In E. Z. Rothkopf (Ed.), *Review of research in education* (Vol. 13) (pp. 49–90). Washington, DC: American Educational Research Association.

Graves, M. F. (1987). The role of instruction in vocabulary development. In M. G. McKeown & M. E. Curtis (Eds.), *The nature of vocabulary acquisition* (pp. 165–184). Hillsdale, NJ: Erlbaum.

Graves, M. F. (1992). The elementary vocabulary curriculum: What should it be? In M. J. Dreher & W. H. Slater (Eds.), *Elementary school literacy: Critical issues* (pp. 101–131). Norwood, MA: Christopher-Gordon.

Graves, M. F. (2000). A vocabulary program to complement and bolster a middle-grade comprehension program. In B. M. Taylor, M. F. Graves, & P. van den Broek (Eds.), *Reading for meaning: Fostering comprehension in the middle grades* (pp. 116–135). New York: Teachers College Press.

Graves, M. F. (2004). Teaching prefixes: As good as it gets?. In J. F. Baumann & E. B. Kame'enui (Eds.), *Vocabulary instruction: Research to practice* (pp. 81–99). New York: Guilford.

Graves, M. F. (2006). *The vocabulary book*. New York: Teachers College Press.

Graves, M. F. (2007). Conceptual and empirical bases for providing struggling readers with multi-faceted and long-term vocabulary instruction. In B. M. Taylor & J. Ysseldyke (Eds.), *Educational perspectives on struggling readers* (pp. 55–83). New York: Teachers College Press.

Graves, M. F., & Gebhart, D. V. (1982). Content teachers' predictions of students' knowledge of specific words. *Reading Psychology, 3,* 211–220.

Graves, M. F., & Graves, B. B. (2003). *Scaffolding reading experiences: Designs for student success* (2nd ed.). Norwood, MA: Christopher-Gordon.

Graves, M. F., Sales, G. C., & Ruda, M. (2008). *The first 4,000 words*. Minneapolis: Seward Inc. Available at thefirst4000words.com.

Graves, M. F., & Slater, W. H. (2008). Vocabulary instruction in the content areas. In D. Lapp, J. Flood, & N. Farnan (Eds.), *Content area reading and learning* (3rd ed.) (pp. 425–447). Mahwah, NJ: Erlbaum.

Gwynne, F. (1970). *The king who rained*. New York: Simon & Schuster.

Haggard, M. R. (1986). The vocabulary self-collection strategy: Using student interest and word knowledge to enhance vocabulary growth. *Journal of Reading, 29,* 634–642.

Hart, B., & Risley, T. R. (1995). *Meaningful differences in the everyday experiences of young American children*. Baltimore: Brookes.

Hart, B., & Risley, T. R. (2003, Spring). The early catastrophe: The 30 million word gap. *American Educator, 27* (1), 4–9.

Hartman, G. W. (1946). Further evidence of the unexpected large size of recognition vocabularies among college students. *Journal of Educational Psychology, 37,* 436–439.

Hayes, D. P., & Ahrens, M. (1988). Vocabulary simplification for children: A special case of "motherese"? *Journal of Child Language, 15,* 395–410.

Heimlich, J. E., & Pittelman, S. D. (1986). *Semantic mapping: Classroom applications.* Newark, DE: International Reading Association.

Herman, P. A., & Dole, J. (1988). Theory and practice in vocabulary learning and instruction. *Elementary School Journal, 89,* 43–54.

Hiebert, E. H. (2005). In pursuit of an effective, efficient vocabulary program. In E. H. Hiebert & M. Kamil (Eds.), *Teaching and learning vocabulary: Bringing research to practice* (pp. 243–263). Mahwah, NJ: Erlbaum.

Hiebert, E. H., & Lubliner, S. (in press). The nature, learning, and instruction of general academic vocabulary. In S. J. Samuels & A. Farstrup (Eds.), *What research has to say about vocabulary.* Newark, DE: International Reading Association.

Hobbs, W. (2006). *Crossing the wire.* New York: HarperCollins.

Hoffman, M. (1986). *Animals in the wild.* Milwaukee: Raintree Children's Press.

Jester, N. (1996). *The phantom tollbooth.* New York: Random House.

Juel, C., & Deffes, R. (2004). Making words stick. *Educational Leadership, 61*(6),30–34.

Kearns, G., & Biemiller, A. (2007, November). *Validation of a new vocabulary assessment method for preliterate students in grades K–2.* Paper presented at the annual meeting of the National Reading Conference, Austin, TX.

Keats, E. J. (1996). *The snowy day.* New York: Viking.

Khalsa, D. K. (1989). *Julian.* Montreal: Tundra Books.

Lee, H. (1995). *To kill a mockingbird.* New York: HarperCollins.

Lionni. L. (1969). *Alexander and the wind-up mouse.* New York: Scholastic.

Lionni, L. (1986). *It's mine!* New York: Knopf.

Longman Study Dictionary of American English. (2006). Essex, UK: Pearson Education Limited.

Lorge, I., & Chall, J. (1963). Estimating the size of vocabularies of children and adults: An analysis of methodological issues. *Journal of Experimental Education, 32,* 147–157.

Lowery, L. (2002). *One more valley, one more hill.* New York: Random House.

MacGinitie, W. H., MacGinitie, R. K., Maria, K., Dreyer, L. G., & Hughes, K. E. (2000). *Gates-MacGinitie reading tests* (4th ed.). Itasca, IL: Riverside Publishing Company.

McLellan, S. S. (2000). *The chicken cat.* Marham, Ontario: Fitzhenry and Whitside.

Microsoft Word 2004 for Mac. (2004). Redmond, WA: Microsoft Corporation.

Miller, G. A. (1956). The magic number seven, plus or minus two: Some limits on our capacity for processing information. *The Psychological Review, 63,* 81–97.

Miller, G. A., & Wakefield, P. C. (1993). Commentary on Anglin's analysis of vocabulary growth. In J. M Anglin, Vocabulary development: A morphological analysis. *Monographs of the Society for Research in Child Development, 59*(10), 167–175.

Morrow, L. M., & Brittain, R. (2003). The nature of storybook reading in the elementary school: Current practices. In A. Stahl & E. B. Bauer (Eds.), *On reading books to children* (pp. 140–158). Mahwah, NJ: Erlbaum.

Murphy, J. (1984). *What next, baby bear!* New York: Dial Books for Young Readers.

Nagy, W. E. (1988). *Teaching vocabulary to improve reading comprehension.* Newark, DE: International Reading Association.

Nagy, W. E. (2005). Why vocabulary instruction needs to be long-term and comprehensive. In E. Hiebert & M. Kamil (Eds.), *Bringing scientific research to practice: Vocabulary* (pp. 27–44). Mahwah, NJ: Erlbaum.

Nagy, W. E., & Anderson, R. C. (1984). How many words are there in printed school English? *Reading Research Quarterly, 19,* 304–330.

Nagy, W. E., & Herman, P. A. (1987). Breadth and depth of vocabulary knowledge: Implications for acquisition and instruction. In M. C. McKeown & M. E. Curtis (Eds.), *The nature of vocabulary acquisition* (pp. 19–35). Hillsdale, NJ: Erlbaum.

Nagy, W. E., Herman, P. A., & Anderson, R.C. (1985). Learning words from context. *Reading Research Quarterly, 20,* 233–253.

Nagy, W. E., & Hiebert, E. H. (2007). *On selecting the right words for vocabulary instruction.* Paper presented at the annual meeting of the National Reading Conference, Austin, TX.

Nagy, W. E., & Scott, J. A. (2000). Vocabulary processes. In M. Kamil, P. Mosenthal, P. D. Pearson & R. Barr (Eds.), *Handbook of reading research* (Vol. 3) (pp. 269–284). New York: Longman.

Osofsky, A. (1996). *Free to dream: The making of a poet: Langston Hughes.* New York: Lothrop, Lee, & Shephard.

Pearson, P. D., & Gallagher, M. C. (1983). The instruction of reading comprehension. *Contemporary Educational Psychology, 8,* 317–344.

Pearson, P. D., Hiebert, E. H., & Kamil, M. (2007). Vocabulary assessment: What we know and what we need to learn. *Reading Research Quarterly, 42,* 282–296.

Perkins, D. N. (1986). *Knowledge as design.* Hillsdale, NJ: Erlbaum.

Perkins, D. N. (1994). *Knowledge as design: A handbook for critical and creative discussion across the curriculum.* Pacific Grove, CA: Critical Thinking Press.

Petty, W., Herold, C., & Stoll, E. (1967). *The state of knowledge about the teaching of vocabulary.* Urbana, IL: National Council of Teachers of English.

Phythian-Sence, C., & Wagner, R. K. (2007). Vocabulary acquisition: A primer. In R. K. Wagner, A. E. Muse, & K. R. Tannenbaum (Eds.), *Vocabulary acquisition: Implications for reading comprehension* (pp. 1–14). New York: Guilford.

Pittelman, S. D., Heimlich, J. E., Berglund, R. L., & French, M. P. (1991). *Semantic feature analysis: Classroom applications.* Newark, DE: International Reading Association.

Read together, talk together parent video. (2002). New York: Pearson Early Learning.

Read together, talk together teacher training video. (2002). New York: Pearson Early Learning.

Richek, M. A. (2005). Words are wonderful: Interactive, time-efficient strategies to teach meaning vocabulary. *The Reading Teacher, 58,* 414–423.

Ruddell, M. R., & Shearer, B. A. (2002). "Extraordinary," "tremendous," "exilarating," "magnificent": Middle school at-risk students become avid word learners with the Vocabulary Self-Collection Strategy (VSS). *Journal of Adolescent and Adult Literacy, 45,* 352–363.

Sachar, L. (1998). *Holes.* New York: Farrar, Straus, and Giroux.

Schertle, A. (1995). *Down the road.* San Diego: Brownder.

Schwartz, R. M., & Raphael, T. E. (1985). Concept of definition: A key to improving students' vocabulary. *The Reading Teacher, 39,* 198–205.

Shibles, B. H. (1959). How many words does the first grade child know? *Elementary English, 31,* 42–47.

Silverman, R. (2007). A comparison of three methods of vocabulary instruction during read-alouds in kindergarten. *Elementary School Journal, 108,* 97–113

Slavin, R. E., & Cheung, A. (2003). *Effective reading programs for English language learners: A best-evidence synthesis.* Baltimore, MD: Johns Hopkins University, Center for the Education of Students Placed at Risk.

Snow, C. E., & Kim, Y. (2007). Large problem spaces: The challenge of vocabulary for English language learners. In R. K. Wagner, A. E. Muse, & K. R. Tasnnenbaum (Eds.), *Vocabulary acquisition: Implications for reading comprehension* (pp. 123–139). New York: Guilford.

Stahl, S. A. (1998). Four questions about vocabulary. In C. R. Hynd (Ed.), *Learning from text across conceptual domains* (pp. 73–94). Mahwah, NJ: Erlbaum.

Stahl, S. A., & Fairbanks, M. M. (1986). The effects of vocabulary instruction: A model-based meta-analysis. *Review of Educational Research, 56,* 72–110.

Stahl, S. A., & Kapinus, B. (1991). Possible sentences: Predicting word meanings to teach content area vocabulary. *The Reading Teacher, 45,* 36–43.

Stahl, S. A., & Nagy, W. (2006). *Teaching word meanings.* Mahwah, NJ: Erlbaum.

Stahl, S. A., & Stahl, K. D. (2004). Word wizards all!: Teaching word meanings in preschool and primary education. In J. F. Baumann & E. B. Kame'enui (Eds.), *Vocabulary instruction: Research to practice* (pp. 59–78). New York: Guilford.

Steinbeck, J. (2002). *The pearl.* New York: Penguin.

Stock, C. (2004). *A spree in Paree.* New York: Holiday House.

Teale, W. H. (2003). Reading aloud to young children as a classroom instructional activity. In A. van Kleeck, S. A. Stahl, & E. B. Bauer (Eds.), *On reading books to children* (pp. 114–139). Mahwah, NJ: Erlbaum.

Templin, M. C. (1957). *Certain language skills in children, their development and interrelationships*. Minneapolis: University of Minnesota Press.

Viorst, J. (1994). *The alphabet from Z to A (with much confusion on the way)*. New York: Macmillan.

Vygotsky, L. S. (1978). *Mind in society: The development of higher psychological processes*. Cambridge, MA: Harvard University Press.

Weizman, Z. O., & Snow, C. E. (2001). Lexical imput as related to children's vocabulary acquisition: Effects of sophisticated exposure and support for meaning. *Developmental Psychology, 37*, 265–279.

White, T. G., Graves, M. F. & Slater, W. H. (1990). Growth of reading vocabulary in diverse elementary schools: Decoding and word meaning. *Journal of Educational Psychology, 82*, 281–290.

White, T. G., Slater, W. H., & Graves, M .F. (1989). Yes/no method of vocabulary assessment: Valid for whom and useful for what? In S. McCormick & J. Zutell (Eds.), *Cognitive and social perspectives for literacy research and instruction* (pp. 391–398). Chicago: National Reading Conference.

Whitehurst, G. J., Arnold, D. S., Epstein, J. N., Angell, A. L., Smith, M., & Fischel, J. E. (1994). A picture book reading intervention in day care and home for children from low-income families. *Developmental Psychology, 30*, 697–689.

Whitehurst, G. J., Falcon, F., Lonigan, C. J., Fischel, J. E., DeBaryshe, D. B., Valdez-Menchaca, M. C., & Caulfield, M. (1988). Accelerating language development through picture book reading. *Developmental Psychology, 24*, 552–559.

Wiggins, G., & McTighe, J. (2005). *Understanding by design* (2nd ed.). Upper Saddle River, NJ: Merrill/Prentice Hall.

Wiske, M. S. (1998). *Teaching for understanding: Linking research with practice*. San Francisco: Jossey-Bass.

Wittgenstein, L. (1953). *Philosophical investigations*. New York: Macmillan.

Zeno, S. M., Ivens, S. H., Millard, R. T., & Duvvuri, R. (1995). *The educator's word frequency guide*. Brewster, NY: Touchstone Applied Science Associates.

Zevenbergen, A. A., & Whitehurst, G. J. (2003). Dialogic reading: A shared picture book reading intervention for preschoolers. In A. V. Kleeck, S. A. Stahl, & E. B. Bauer (Eds.), *On reading books to children: Parents and teachers* (pp. 177–200). Mahwah, NJ: Erlbaum.

Index

Accommodations
  general accommodations for English
      learners, 30–31
  when teaching individual words, 31–32
Ahrens, M., 34, 37
Alexander and the Wind-Up Mouse (Lionni),
  42
American English. *See also* English learners
  dialects of students and, 4
  frequency distribution of words in, 20–23,
      37
  number of words in, 13–14
American Heritage Word Frequency Book, The
  (Carroll et al.), 13–14
Analytic Instruction (Silverman), 39
Anchored Instruction (Juel and Deffes), 39
Anderson, R. C., 13–15, 34
Angell, A. L., 39
Anglin, J. M., 15
Anything Goes procedure, 81–82
Arnold, D. S., 39
Asian/Pacific students, dialect-speaking
  by, 4
Assessing word knowledge, 85–90
  Gates-MacGinitie Reading Tests, 88–89
  multiple-choice items, 89–90
  Peabody Picture Vocabulary Test IV
      (PPVT-4), 85–86, 87
  student self-reporting, 90
  Two-Sentence Procedure (Kern and Bi-
      emiller), 86–88
August, D., 30

Baker, S., 30
Baldwin, L. E., 4–5
Beck, I. L., 12, 27, 35, 39, 60, 66–67, 81, 84
Becker, W. C., 4
Becoming a Nation of Readers (Anderson et
  al.), 34
Berglund, R. L., 49–51

Biemiller, A., 5, 15, 23–24, 27, 39, 42–44, 85,
  86–88
Birdwell, Norman, 42
Blachowicz, C. L. Z., 58–60
Black students, dialect-speaking by, 4
Blind students, 1–2
Boote, C., 5, 42–43
Brittain, R., 34

Calfee, R. C., 13
Carroll, J. B., 4, 13–14
Caulfield, M., 39
Chall, J. S., 4–5, 14–15
Cheung, A., 30
Chicken Cat, The (McLellan), 42
Clifford at the Circus (Birdwell), 42
Collins COBUILD New Student's Dictionary,
  30
Competence, vocabulary and, 3
Complimenting students, 36
Comprehensive vocabulary program, 5–7
  extensive language experiences in, 6
  frequent language experiences in, 6
  individual words in, 6–7
  varied language experiences in, 6
  word consciousness in, 7
  word-learning strategies in, 7, 10–18
  Connect Two procedure, 82–83
Context analysis skills, 26
Context-Dictionary-Discussion procedure,
  72
Context-Relationship procedure, 74–76
Cronbach, L. J., 13
Crossing the Wire (Hobbs), 89
Cummins, J., 30

Dale, E., 24, 25
Davies, P., 13–14
Deaf students, 1–2
DeBaryshe, D. B., 39

Decoding, 70
Deffes, R., 39
Definition, Rich Context, and a Picture pro-
    cedure, 73–74, 75
Definition Plus Rich Context procedure,
    72–73
Definitions
  student-friendly, 29–30
  traditional, 29
De Temple, J., 37, 38
Dialects, 4
Dialogic Reading, 39–41
  described, 39–40
  example of, 41
  procedures used with, 40–41
  prompts used in, 40
  teaching procedure for, 43–44
  videotapes on, 41
Differences across grade levels, 6, 90–92
Discussion
  Focused Discussion, 57–58
  topics that invite sophisticated vocabu-
      lary, 36–37
Dole, J., 27
Down the Road (Schertle), 42
Dreyer, L. G., 88–89
Drum, P. A., 13
Duin, A. H., 66–67, 85
Dunn, D. M., 85–86
Dunn, L. M., 85–86
Dupuy, H., 14
Duvvuri, R., 14, 20, 22

Educator's Word Frequency Guide, The (Zeno
    et al.), 14, 20
Eighth grade, Vocabulary Self-Collection
    Strategy in, 56
Elementary grades, vocabulary instruction
    in, 6
Encouraging students, 36
English language
  American English, 4, 13–14, 20–23, 37
  frequency distribution of words in, 20–23,
      37
English learners, 3. *See also* American Eng-
    lish
  accommodations when teaching individ-
      ual words, 31–32
  general accommodations for, 30–31
  generalizations concerning, 30
  oral vocabulary development for students

  with small vocabularies, 37–44
  special considerations for, 30–32
Epstein, J. N., 39
Expressive Vocabulary Instruction, 18,
    66–67
  described, 66
  sample student essay, 68
  steps in, 66–67
Extensive language experiences, 6

Fairbanks, M. M., 27
Falcon, F., 39
Finger spelling, 1–2
First grade
  vocabulary knowledge in, 3
  Words in Context and, 43
First 4,000 Words, The (Graves et al.), 23–24,
    85, 89
Fischel, J. E., 39
Fitzgerald, J., 31
Focused Discussion, 57–58
  described, 57
  steps in, 57–58
Four Squares, 51–53, 91
  described, 51
  examples of, 52
  steps in, 51–52
Frayer, D. A., 64–66
Frayer Method, 63–66
  described, 64
  steps in, 64–66
  strengths of, 66
Frederick, W. D., 64–66
French, M. P., 49–51
Frequency distribution
  of English words, 20–23, 37
  of rare words in various sources, 37
Frequent language experiences, 6

Gallagher, M. C., 66
Gates-MacGinitie Reading Tests, 88–89
Gebhart, D. V., 24
Gersten, R., 30
Giblin, J. C., 20, 22
Gillman, Phoebe, 42
Glossaries, 89
  Providing Glossaries procedure, 70–71
Goldenberg, C., 30
Graves, B. B., 35
Graves, M. F., 3–5, 7, 14–15, 23, 24, 26, 31,
    35, 66–67, 74–76, 85, 89–90

Haggard, M. R., 53
Hart, B., 5, 15
Hartman, G. W., 14
Hayes, D. P., 34, 37
Heimlich, J. E., 47–48, 49–51
Herman, P. A., 15, 27
Herold, C., 2
Hiebert, E. H., 20, 23, 34, 85
Hobbs, Will, 89
Hughes, K. E., 88–89

Incremental learning, 13
Instructional procedures
   Context-Dictionary-Discussion, 72
   Context-Relationship, 74–76
   Definition, Rich Context, and a Picture,
      73–74, 75
   Definition Plus Rich Context, 72–73
   Dialogic Reading, 39–41
   differences across grade levels, 6, 90–92
   Expressive Vocabulary Instruction, 18,
      66–67
   Focused Discussion, 57–58
   Four Squares, 51–53, 91
   Frayer Method, 64–66
   introductory, 69–78
   Knowledge as Design, 62–64
   oral vocabulary development for all stu-
      dents, 34–37
   oral vocabulary development for students
      with small vocabularies, 37–44
   Possible Sentences, 55–57, 91
   Providing Glossaries, 70–71
   repetition-based, 80–85
   Robust Instruction, 60–61
   Semantic Feature Analysis, 49–51
   Semantic Mapping, 47–49
   shared book reading, 37–44
   Teaching New Meanings for Known
      Words, 76–77
   Teaching Students to Read Known Words,
      70, 91
   Venn Diagrams, 53, 54
   Vocabulary Self-Collection Strategy,
      53–55, 56
   Vocabulary Visits, 58–60
   Words in Context, 39, 42–44
Intermediate grades
   differences across grade levels, 6, 91
   frequency distribution of words and,
      21–22

vocabulary instruction in, 6
Introductory instructional procedures,
   69–78
   Context-Dictionary-Discussion, 72
   Context-Relationship, 74–76
   Definition, Rich Context, and a Picture,
      73–74, 75
   Definition Plus Rich Context, 72–73
   Providing Glossaries, 70–71
   Teaching New Meanings for Known
      Words, 76–77
   Teaching Students to Read Known Words,
      70, 91
Ivens, S. H., 14, 20, 22

Jacobs, V. A., 4–5
Jillian Jiggs (Gillman), 42
Johnson, Lyndon, 2
Juel, C., 39
Julian (Khalsa), 42

Kamil, M., 85
Kapinus, B., 55–57
Kearns, G., 86–88
Keats, Ezra Jack, 41
Keller, Helen, 1–2, 9
Khalsa, Dayal, 42
Kim, Y., 15
Kindergarten
   vocabulary instruction in, 6
   vocabulary knowledge in, 3
   Words in Context and, 43
Klausmeier, H. J., 64–66
Knowledge as Design, 62–64
   described, 62
   sample worksheet, 63
   steps in, 62–63
Known words
   clarifying and enriching meanings of,
      17–18
   levels of knowledge of, 12–13
   new meanings for, 17, 76–77
   reading, 16, 70, 91
   Teaching New Meanings for Known
      Words procedure, 76–77
   Teaching Students to Read Known Words
      procedure, 70, 91
Kucan, L., 12, 27, 35, 60, 84

Lexicon, English, 20
Lindbergh, Charles, 20–22

Lionni, Leo, 42
Listening, word learning through, 35–36
Living Word Vocabulary, The (Dale and O'Rourke), 24–25
Longman Study Dictionary of American English, 30
Lonigan, C. J., 39
Lorge, L., 14–15
Lubliner, S., 23

MacGinitie, R. K., 88–89
MacGinitie, W. H., 88–89
Maria, K., 88–89
McKeown, M. G., 12, 27, 35, 39, 60, 66–67, 81, 84
McLellan, Stephanie, 42
McTighe, J., 37
Middle grades
  differences across grade levels, 6, 91–92
  vocabulary instruction in, 6
Millard, R. T., 14, 20, 22
Miller, George A., 15, 92
Morrow, L. M., 34
Multiple-choice assessment, 89–90
Murphy, Jill, 38

Nagy, W. E., 13–15, 23, 27, 51–53, 57–58
New meanings, for known words, 17
New words
  identifying unknown words, 23–26
  representing known concepts, 16–17
  representing new concepts, 17
  sources of, 23–26

Obrochte, C., 58–60
Oral vocabulary, 33–45
  approaches for all students, 34–37
  approach for students with small vocabularies, 37–44
  complimenting student use of adept word choices, 36
  encouraging student use of adept word choices, 36
  learning basic, 16
  reading aloud to children, 34–35
  reading vocabulary versus, 11–12, 15
  shared book reading for, 37–44
  sophisticated language use by teachers, 35–36
  topics that invite sophisticated vocabulary, 36–37

O'Rourke, J., 24, 25

Peabody Picture Vocabulary Test IV (PPVT-4), 85–86, 87
Pearson, P. D., 66, 85
Perfetti, C. A., 60, 81, 84
Perkins, D. N., 62
Petty, W., 2
Phythian-Sence, C., 3
Pittelman, S. D., 47–48, 49–51
Possible Sentences, 55–57, 91
  described, 55–56
  sample words selected in, 56–57
  steps in, 56
Poverty, vocabulary and, 3, 4–5
Primary grades, differences across grade levels, 6, 91
Productive vocabulary, 11
Project Follow Through, 4
Providing Glossaries procedure, 70–71

Raphael, T. E., 51–52
Readability of text, 3
Reading aloud to children, 34–35
Reading comprehension, 3
Reading vocabulary
  identifying unknown words, 25
  oral vocabulary versus, 11–12, 15
  reading aloud to children and, 34–35
  reading known words in, 16, 70, 91
  shared book reading and, 37–44
Read Together, Talk Together Parent Video (videotape), 41
Read Together, Talk Together Teacher Training Video (videotape), 41
Receptive vocabulary, 11
Repetition, 80–85
  Anything Goes procedure, 81–82
  Connect Two procedure, 82–83
  importance of, 80–81
  Two in One procedure, 83–84
  Word Wizard procedure, 84–85
Richek, M. A., 81–83, 85
Richman, B., 13–14
Risley, T. R., 5, 15
Robust Instruction, 60–61
  described, 60
  steps in, 60–61
Ruda, M., 23, 85, 89–90
Ruddell, M. R., 53–55

Sales, G. C., 23, 85, 89–90
Scaffolding, in shared book reading, 38
Schertle, Alice, 42
School failure, 3
School success, vocabulary and, 4
Schwartz, R. M., 51–52
Scott, J. A., 13, 34
Second grade, Words in Context and, 43
Self-reporting by students, 90
Semantic Feature Analysis, 49–51
  described, 49
  examples of, 49, 51
  steps in, 50–51
Semantic Mapping, 47–49
  described, 47–48
  examples of, 48
  key features of, 49
Sensory deprivation, 1–2
Shanahan, T., 30
Shared book reading, 37–44
  characteristics of, 38–39
  Dialogic Reading, 39–41
  Words in Context, 39, 42–44
Shearer, B. A., 53–55
Shibles, B. H., 14
Silverman, R., 39
Slater, W. H., 4, 15, 26, 74–76, 90
Slavin, R. E., 30
Slonim, N., 15
Smith, M., 39
Snow, C. E., 15, 30, 37, 38
Snowy Day, The (Keats), 41
Sophisticated language
  topics that invite use of, 36–37
  use by teachers, 35–36
Stahl, K. D., 3, 34
Stahl, S. A., 3, 15, 27, 34, 51–52, 55–57
Stoll, E., 2
Structural analysis skills, 26
Student-friendly definitions, 29–30
  defined, 29
  examples of, 29
  importance of, 29–30
  sources of, 29–30
Sullivan, Anne, 1–2

Teaching for Understanding (Wiske), 37
Teaching New Meanings for Known Words
    procedure, 76–77
Teaching Students to Read Known Words
    procedure, 70, 91

Teale, W. H., 34–35
Templin, M. C., 15
Text Talk (Beck and McKeown), 39
Tier 2 words (Beck et al.), 27, 35–36
Traditional definitions, 29
Two in One procedure, 83–84
Two-Sentence Procedure (Kern and Biemiller), 86–88

Understanding by Design (Wiggins and McTighe), 37

Valdez-Menchaca, M. C., 39
Varied language experiences, 6
Venn Diagrams
  described, 53
  examples of, 54
Vocabulary Book, The (Graves), 7
Vocabulary instruction. *See also* Instructional procedures; Word learning
  assessment in, 85–90
  comprehensive four-part program for, 5–7
  data-based claims for, 3
  differences across grade levels, 6, 90–92
  frequency distribution of English words, 20–23, 37
  frequency of rare words in various sources, 37
  importance of, 2–3
  for linguistically less advantaged children, 3–5
  oral vocabulary in, 33–45
  principles of effective, 27–29
  selecting vocabulary to teach, 23–27
  sensory deprivation and, 1–2
  size of vocabulary, 12
  special considerations for English learners, 30–32
  student-friendly definitions in, 29–30
  traditional definitions in, 29
Vocabulary Self-Collection Strategy, 53–55
  described, 53
  sample words selected in, 56
  steps in, 55
Vocabulary Visits, 58–60
  described, 58
  sample words for, 60
  steps in, 58–59
Vygotsky, L. S., 40

Wagner, R. K., 3

Wakefield, P. C., 15
Weizman, Z. O., 38
What Next, Baby Bear! (Murphy), 38
White, T. G., 4, 15, 26, 90
Whitehurst, G. J., 39–41
Wiggins, G., 37
Wilkinson, I. A. G., 34
Williams, Robin, 36
Wiske, M. S., 37
Wittgenstein, Ludwig, 2
Word consciousness, in vocabulary instruction, 7
Word learning, 7, 10–18. See also Instructional procedures; Vocabulary instruction
 differences across grade levels, 6, 90–92
 frequency distribution of English words, 20–23, 37
 identifying unknown words, 23–26
 "knowing" a word, 12–13
 levels of knowledge in, 12–13
 nature of words, 11–12
 number of vocabularies, 11

number of words in American English, 13–14
number of words learned by students, 14–15
reading aloud to children and, 34–35
selecting words to teach, 26–27
shared book reading and, 37–44
tasks in, 15–18
Word lists, 23–25
Words in Context, 39, 42–44
 books appropriate for, 42
 described, 42
 word selection for, 42–43
Words Worth Teaching (Biemiller), 23–24
Words Worth Teaching in Grades Three-Six (Biemiller), 85
Word Wizard procedure, 84–85
Word Zones™ (Hiebert), 20–22, 23

Zeno, S. M., 14, 20, 22
Zevenbergen, A. A., 39–41
Zone of proximal development, 40

About the Author

Michael F. Graves is Professor Emeritus of Literacy Education at the University of Minnesota and a member of the Reading Hall of Fame. He has served as the editor of the *Journal of Reading Behavior* and as the associate editor of *Research in the Teaching of English*. His most recent books are *Fostering Comprehension in English Classes* (with Raymond Philippot, 2009), *Teaching Reading in the 21st Century* (4th edition, with Connie Juel & Bonnie Graves, 2007), *Reading and Responding in the Middle Grades* (with Lee Galda, 2007), and *The Vocabulary Book* (2006).